AF528527

Preface

The fields of Data Science and Big Data have become cornerstones of modern technology and business, revolutionizing the way organizations operate, make decisions, and drive innovation. As industries across the globe increasingly rely on data to gain insights and maintain competitive advantages, the demand for skilled professionals in Data Science and Big Data has soared. Recognizing this, IGNOU offers a comprehensive course designed to equip students with the theoretical knowledge and practical skills required to excel in these dynamic and rapidly evolving fields.

This book, "IGNOU Data Science and Big Data: Previous Years Unsolved Papers," has been meticulously compiled to serve as a vital resource for students pursuing this course. The collection of previous years' unsolved papers included in this book is intended to provide students with a clear understanding of the exam format, the variety of questions posed, and the key topics that have been emphasized in past assessments. These papers are an invaluable tool for students to practice and hone their problem-solving skills, gain familiarity with the types of challenges they may encounter in exams, and identify areas where further study may be needed.

By working through these unsolved papers, students are not merely preparing for their exams; they are also deepening their understanding of the core principles and advanced techniques of Data Science and Big Data. Each question in these papers has been designed to test not just knowledge, but the ability to apply concepts to real-world problems, analyse data critically, and derive meaningful conclusions—skills that are essential for any aspiring data scientist or big data professional.

This collection also serves to encourage students to think analytically and develop a mindset geared toward innovation and discovery. In the fast-paced world of data, where new tools and methodologies are constantly emerging, the ability to think critically and adapt to new challenges is as important as the foundational knowledge itself.

Moreover, these unsolved papers provide an opportunity for students to simulate exam conditions, allowing them to manage their time effectively and develop strategies for tackling difficult questions under pressure. This practice is invaluable in building the confidence needed to approach exams with a calm and focused mindset.

We believe that this book will not only be a key element in your exam preparation but also a significant aid in your overall academic and professional journey. By engaging deeply with the material presented here, you will be better equipped to meet the demands of the Data Science and Big Data fields and to contribute meaningfully to the ever-growing landscape of data-driven innovation.

Whether you are preparing for your upcoming exams, revising key concepts, or seeking to challenge yourself with complex problems, this collection of unsolved papers will serve as a trusted guide and companion. We encourage you to approach these papers with diligence and curiosity, and we wish you success in your studies and beyond.

Table of Contents

Master Of Computer Applications (MCA)
Chapter 1: Term-End Examinations, June, 2022
MCS-226: Data Science and Big Data

Time: 3 Hours
Maximum Marks: 100
Weightage: 70

Note: Question No. 1 is compulsory. Answer any three Questions from the rest.

1. (a) What is the Data Science ? What are its applications ? Explain the terms categorical and quantitative data with the help of an example for each. 5
(b) Assume that a fair coin is tossed 4 times. What would be the probability distribution of a variable X, which represents the number of tails in bur tosses of coin ? What kind of probability distribution is this ? Justify. 5
(c) What is Big data ? Explain the characteristics of Big data. 5
(d) What is the map-reduce paradigm ? Explain with the help of an example. 5
(e) Define the term similarity. Explain the Jaccard similarity of sets with the help of an example. 5
(f) What is a data stream ? How is data stream processing different from transaction processing ? 5
(g) Write a program using R to add and subtract two matrices. 5
(h) Define the term classification, Write the steps about how R programming can be used to perform claseification. 5

2. (a) What are the different measures for defining the spread of a quantitative variable ? Explain. 5
(b) What is meant by 'Sampling Distribution' ? Explain with the help of an example. 5
(c) Explain the concept of data pre-processing and data cleaning with tbc help of an example each. 5
(d) What is a box plot ? Draw a sample box plot and explain it. 5

3. (a) Explain the characteristics of HDFS. What are tho advantages of HDFS over file allocation table (FAT) based system ? 5
(b) What is the role of shuffing and sorting in map-reduce ? Explain with the help of an example. 5
(c) What are the features of SPARK architecture ? Explain. 5
(d) What are NoSQL databases ? How are they from relational database system ? 5

4. (a) What is collaborative filtering ? Explain with the help of an example. 5.
(b) What is the use of Bloom filtering ? Explain with the help of an example. 5
(c) Explain Any page ranking algorithm with the help of an example. 5
(d) Explain the issues related to mining of social networks. 5

5. (a) Define the following in the context of R programming, with the help of an example : 5
(i) Complex data type
(ii) % % operator
(iii) ← or <<- operator
(iv) Vectors
(v) Strings

(b) What is the use of bar chart ? How can you draw a bar chart using R programming language ? Explain. 5
(c) What is linear regression ? Explain how R programming can be used to perform linear regression. 5
(d) What is clustering ? Write the steps of how R-programming can be used to perform K-mean clustering. What is confusion matrix in this context ? 5

Master Of Computer Applications (MCA)
Chapter 2: Term-End Examination, December, 2022
MCS-226: Data Science and Big Data

Time: 3 Hours
Maximum Marks: 100
Weightage: 70

Note: (i) Question No. 1 is compulsory.
(ii) Answer any three Questions from the rest.

1. (a) Explain the following types of data : 6
(i) Semi-structured data
(ii) Unstructured data
(iii) Qualitative data
(iv) Quantitative data

(b) What is meant by "Probability distribution of continuous random variable" ? Explain with the help of a diagram. Also explain the normal distribution. 6

(c) What are the characteristics of Hadoop Distributed File System (HDFS) ? Why is it used for Big data processing? 6

(d) Explain the characteristics of data streams. 4

(e) What are NoSQL databases ? Why are they used ? 4

(f) Explain any one mechanism of filtering of data streams. 4

(g) Explain the following, with the help of an example, in the context of R programming: 6
(i) Dataframe
(ii) List
(iii) Vector

(h) What is logistic regression ? Which function of R programming can be used to implement logistic regression? 4

2. (a) Explain the characteristics of measurement scales of data. Use these characteristics to define various measurement scales of data. 6

(b) Explain the steps of significance testing, with the help of an example. 8

(c) Explain the following terms with the help of an example : 6
(i) Data pre-processing
(ii) Data curation
(iii) Data cleaning

3. (a) Explain the characteristics of Big data. How does Big data differ from relational data ? 6

(b) Explain the steps of map-reduce paradigm using the example of word counting. 6

(c) List the features of any two of the following : 8
(i) Apache Spark
(ii) Hive
(iii) Column-based databases
(iv) Graph-based databases

4. (a) How can link analysis be used to compute PageRank ? 4

(b) Explain the concept of Recommendation System. 6

(c) Explain how the similarity between two documents can be found. 6

(d) Explain how the social networks can be represented using a graph. 4

5. (a) Write an R program to create two 3 x 3 matrices and multiply them. How is this program different from a similar C program ? 5

(b) What is a box plot ? List the commands of R programming that can be used to create a box plot. 5

(c) What is multiple regression ? Write steps about how R programming can be used to create multiple regression model. 5

(d) What is a decision tree ? Write steps on how R programming can be used for making decision tree. 5

Master Of Computer Applications (MCA)
Chapter 3: Term-End Examination, June, 2023
MCS-226: Data Science and Big Data

Time: 3 Hours
Maximum Marks: 100
Weightage: 70
Note: Question No. 1 is compulsory. Answer any three Questions from the rest.

1. (a) Define Data Science. Give advantages of Data Science in an organization. 5

(b) Explain Bayes' Theorem with suitable equation and example. 5

(c) What is a Histogram ? How does Histogram differ from Bargraph ? Briefly discuss the utility of Histogram in Data Science. 5

(d) What is Hadoop MapReduce ? Give its advantages. Also, discuss how <key-value> pair mechanism facilitates MapReduce programming. 5

(e) In context of Data Science, what is Apache SPARK ? How does Apache SPARK differ from Hadoop ? 5

(f) What are Data Streams ? How do Data Streams differ from Databases ? Why mining of data streams is considered as a challenging process in Data Science ? 5

(g) Explain PageRank algorithm, with suitable example. 5

(h) What are Dataframes in 'R' programming ? Give characteristics of Dataframes. 5

2. (a) Write the syntax to create the following plots in 'R' : 5
(i) Bar charts
(ii) Box plots
(iii) Histogram
(iv) Line graphs
(v) Scatter plots

(b) Differentiate between Linear Regression and Multiple Regression, with suitable example for each. 5

(c) What are Decision Trees ? What are categorical variables and continuous variables ? How do these two variables relate to decision trees ? Explain the role of entropy and information gain in decision trees. 10

3. (a) Compare qualitative data with quantitative data. What do you understand by the term "Measurement scale of data" ? Give characteristics of measurement scales of data. List various measurement scales with suitable example for each. 10

(b) What is a Random Variable ? Differentiate between Discrete Random Variable and Continuous Random Variable. 5

(c) What is a Heat Map ? Give uses and best practices for Heat Maps. 5

4. (a) Explain the following operations of map-reduce with suitable example and supporting block diagram : 10

(i) Splitting
(ii) Mapping
(iii) Shuffling

(iv) Reducing

(b) Explain the term Data lake. Briefly discuss the key capabilities of data lake. 5

(c) Compare Land Mark Model and Sliding Windows Model for data stream processing. 5

5. Write short notes on the following : $4 \times 5 = 20$

(a) Different mechanisms of finding PageRank

(b) Chi-square test

(c) Association Rules

(d) Predictive Analysis

(e) HIVE and its utility in Data Science

Master Of Computer Applications (MCA)
Chapter 4: Term-End Examination, December, 2023
MCS-226: Data Science and Big Data

Time: 3 Hours
Maximum Marks: 100
Weightage: 70
Note: (i) Question No. 1 is compulsory. Answer any three Questions from the rest.

1. (a) How does sampling differ from population ? Also, discuss the relation of the terms 'statistic' and 'parameter', with sampling and population, respectively. 5

(b) What is conditional probability ? Write the equation for conditional probability and describe its components with a suitable example. 5

(c) What is a BoxPlot ? What are whiskers in any BoxPlot ? Briefly discuss the utility of BoxPlots in Data Science. 5

(d) What is MapReduce ? Explain the Map function and Reduce function in the Map-Reduce architecture with a suitable block diagram. 5

(e) What is Apache Spark ? Give main features of Apache Spark framework. 5

(f) Differentiate between Data Stream Management System (DSMS) and Data Base Management System (DBMS). 5

(g) Explain the term 'Link Analysis'. Briefly discuss the purpose of link analysis in data science. How link analysis can be used for World Wide Web (WWW) ? 5

(h) Briefly describe the following data structures of 'R' programming with the help of an example for each : 5

(i) Vector
(ii) List

2. (a) What is Data Cleaning ? List and briefly discuss the best practices used for data cleaning and data preparation. 5

(b) What is Logistic Regression ? Give its utility. Also, write and discuss the function of 'R' used to construct the model for logistic regression. 5

(c) What is a Random Forest ? How does it differ from Decision tree ? Explain the role of partitioning, pruning and tree selection process in the working of decision tree. 10

3. (a) Explain the following types of data, used in data science. Give suitable example for each : 10
(i) Structured data
(ii) Semi-structured data
(iii) Unstructured data
(iv) Data streams

(b) What is Binomial Distribution ? Write the formula for binomial probability distribution and use it to produce the probability distribution for the case of three tosses of the coin. 5

(c) What is a scatter plot ? Give uses and best practices for scatter plot. 5

4. (a) Explain word count problem with suitable example. Give pseudo-code for word count problem in MapReduce. 5

(b) Briefly discuss the purpose of the following components of Apache Spark : 10
(i) Spark core
(ii) Spark SQL
(iii) Spark Streaming
(iv) MLib
(v) Graph X

(c) Compare Ad-hoc Queries and Standing Queries of data streams. Give example for each. 5

5. Write short notes on the following : 4*5=20
(a) Sensitive PageRank
(b) Time series analysis
(c) Clustering and its types in 'R' programming
(d) Data Science life cycle
(e) HBase and its utility in Data Science

Chapter 5: Most Asked Questions Part-A

1. What is Data Science and why is it important?
Answer: Data Science is an interdisciplinary field that uses scientific methods, algorithms, processes, and systems to extract knowledge and insights from structured and unstructured data. It combines statistics, machine learning, data mining, and computer science to analyze large volumes of data for informed decision-making. Data Science is important because it enables organizations to make data-driven decisions, uncover hidden patterns, and gain a competitive advantage. From healthcare and finance to marketing and e-commerce, industries rely on data science to improve services, optimize operations, and predict trends. As the volume of data continues to grow, the demand for skilled data scientists increases globally.

2. What are the key components of Data Science?
Answer: The main components of Data Science include data collection, data cleaning, data analysis, data visualization, and machine learning. Data collection involves gathering raw data from various sources such as databases, APIs, and sensors. Data cleaning ensures the removal of inconsistencies and missing values. Data analysis applies statistical and computational methods to extract insights. Data visualization helps communicate findings through charts and graphs. Machine learning involves building predictive models using algorithms. These components work together to transform raw data into actionable knowledge, making Data Science a powerful tool in solving complex real-world problems across industries.

3. What is Big Data and how does it differ from traditional data?
Answer: Big Data refers to extremely large and complex datasets that cannot be managed, processed, or analyzed using traditional data processing tools. It is characterized by the "3 Vs": Volume (massive amount of data), Velocity (speed at which data is generated and processed), and Variety (diverse data types, including structured, semi-structured, and unstructured). Traditional data typically resides in relational databases and can be handled with basic tools. In contrast, Big Data requires advanced frameworks like Hadoop, Spark, and NoSQL databases. Its ability to store and process massive datasets makes Big Data essential for real-time analytics, trend forecasting, and decision-making.

4. How are Data Science and Big Data connected?
Answer: Data Science and Big Data are closely related but not the same. Big Data provides the massive volume and variety of data, while Data Science provides the tools and techniques to analyze and interpret that data. Data Science uses Big Data technologies to process and extract insights from large datasets. Techniques such as machine learning, predictive analytics, and natural language processing rely on Big Data infrastructure for scalability and speed. Together, they enable organizations to uncover patterns, predict outcomes, and drive innovation. Thus, Big Data fuels the data-driven processes that Data Science aims to explore and optimize.

5. What is the role of a data scientist?
Answer: A data scientist is responsible for collecting, analyzing, and interpreting complex data to help organizations make informed decisions. Their role involves cleaning and preprocessing data, applying statistical models, building machine learning algorithms, and visualizing results. Data scientists also collaborate with domain experts to understand business requirements and deliver insights that drive strategic planning. They must be proficient in programming (e.g., Python, R), data handling tools (e.g., SQL, Pandas), and visualization platforms (e.g., Tableau, Power BI). Their ability to transform raw data into valuable insights makes them essential in sectors like finance, healthcare, retail, and technology.

6. What are the main tools used in Data Science?
Answer: Data Science tools vary across tasks, but commonly used tools include programming languages like Python and R for data analysis and modeling. Jupyter Notebook and RStudio serve as development environments. Pandas, NumPy, and Scikit-learn in Python aid in data manipulation and machine learning. For visualization, tools such as Matplotlib, Seaborn, Tableau, and Power BI are popular. SQL is used for data querying, while Hadoop and Apache Spark handle Big Data processing. Git and GitHub assist in version control and collaboration. These tools streamline the data science workflow, from data collection to model deployment and insight presentation.

7. What is machine learning and how is it used in Data Science?
Answer: Machine learning is a branch of artificial intelligence that enables systems to learn from data and improve

their performance without being explicitly programmed. In Data Science, machine learning is used to build predictive models that can identify trends, classify data, and make forecasts. Supervised learning, unsupervised learning, and reinforcement learning are common types. Applications include spam detection, recommendation systems, fraud detection, and image recognition. By automating analytical model building, machine learning allows data scientists to develop intelligent solutions that evolve with new data, making it a cornerstone of modern data-driven applications.

8. What are structured and unstructured data?
Answer: Structured data refers to data that is organized into rows and columns, typically found in relational databases. It is easily searchable and follows a predefined format, such as customer information or sales records. Unstructured data lacks a fixed structure and includes formats like text documents, images, videos, emails, and social media posts. While structured data is easier to manage and analyze, unstructured data holds immense potential for insights when processed using techniques like natural language processing and image analysis. Data Science relies on both data types to build comprehensive and effective analytical models.

9. What are the top programming languages used in Data Science?
Answer: The top programming languages used in Data Science include Python, R, SQL, and sometimes Java and Scala. Python is the most popular due to its simplicity, large library support (like Pandas, NumPy, Scikit-learn, TensorFlow), and versatility. R is preferred for statistical analysis and academic research. SQL is essential for querying and managing data in relational databases. Java and Scala are often used in Big Data frameworks like Apache Hadoop and Spark. Each language offers unique strengths, and data scientists often choose based on the task at hand and the project requirements.

10. What is the CRISP-DM methodology in Data Science?
Answer: CRISP-DM (Cross-Industry Standard Process for Data Mining) is a widely used methodology that outlines the process for carrying out a data science project. It consists of six phases: Business Understanding, Data Understanding, Data Preparation, Modeling, Evaluation, and Deployment. This iterative framework helps data scientists systematically approach problem-solving by aligning technical tasks with business goals. CRISP-DM ensures that the final model is both technically sound and practically useful. It promotes collaboration among stakeholders, encourages data exploration, and emphasizes model validation and performance analysis before implementation.

11. What is data preprocessing and why is it essential in Data Science?
Answer: Data preprocessing is the technique of transforming raw data into a clean and structured format suitable for analysis. It involves steps like data cleaning, normalization, transformation, handling missing values, and feature selection. Preprocessing is essential because real-world data is often incomplete, noisy, or inconsistent. Without proper preprocessing, models can produce inaccurate results or fail entirely. It ensures that the input data improves the quality of the analysis, enhances model performance, and leads to reliable insights. Thus, data preprocessing is a critical step that influences the success of any data science project.

12. What are the main types of machine learning?
Answer: Machine learning is broadly categorized into three types: supervised learning, unsupervised learning, and reinforcement learning. In supervised learning, models are trained on labeled data to predict outcomes; examples include regression and classification. Unsupervised learning deals with unlabeled data to find hidden patterns, using techniques like clustering and dimensionality reduction. Reinforcement learning involves training agents to make sequences of decisions by rewarding desired behavior. Each type serves different purposes in data science, such as customer segmentation, recommendation systems, or robotic control. Understanding these types helps in selecting the right approach for solving specific problems.

13. What is supervised learning in Data Science?
Answer: Supervised learning is a type of machine learning where the model is trained on a labeled dataset. The goal is to learn the mapping between input variables (features) and output variables (labels) so that the model can make accurate predictions on new data. Common algorithms include Linear Regression, Decision Trees, Support Vector Machines, and Random Forests. Supervised learning is used in applications like spam detection, credit scoring, and image classification. It provides high accuracy when trained on quality data and is widely adopted for predictive modeling in various industries.

14. What is unsupervised learning in Data Science?
Answer: Unsupervised learning is a machine learning technique that analyzes and clusters unlabeled datasets. The model identifies hidden patterns or groupings without prior knowledge of outcomes. Techniques include clustering (e.g., K-means, Hierarchical) and dimensionality reduction (e.g., PCA). It is widely used in market segmentation, anomaly detection, and recommendation systems. Unsupervised learning helps in discovering data structures that are not obvious and enables exploratory analysis. Since there are no correct answers provided during training, evaluating the model's performance often requires domain expertise or additional labeled data.

15. What is reinforcement learning and how does it work?
Answer: Reinforcement learning is a type of machine learning where an agent learns to make decisions by interacting with an environment. The agent takes actions to maximize cumulative rewards over time. It receives feedback in the form of rewards or penalties based on its actions and adjusts its strategy accordingly. Reinforcement learning is used in applications like game playing, robotics, and autonomous vehicles. It involves concepts such as states, actions, policies, and value functions. The goal is to learn an optimal policy that leads to the best long-term outcomes through trial and error.

16. What is the importance of feature selection in machine learning?
Answer: Feature selection is the process of identifying and selecting the most relevant variables or features for building predictive models. It is important because irrelevant or redundant features can reduce model accuracy, increase training time, and lead to overfitting. Feature selection simplifies models, enhances generalization, and makes results easier to interpret. Techniques such as correlation analysis, recursive feature elimination, and mutual information are commonly used. By focusing only on the most impactful features, data scientists can build more efficient and effective models that perform well on new data.

17. What is dimensionality reduction in Data Science?
Answer: Dimensionality reduction is a technique used to reduce the number of input variables in a dataset while preserving essential information. It helps to overcome challenges like overfitting, high computational costs, and visualization issues in high-dimensional data. Common methods include Principal Component Analysis (PCA) and t-Distributed Stochastic Neighbor Embedding (t-SNE). Dimensionality reduction is crucial in fields like image processing, genomics, and natural language processing. By simplifying the dataset, it improves model performance and interpretability while retaining the underlying structure and patterns within the data.

18. What is data visualization and why is it important?
Answer: Data visualization is the graphical representation of information and data through charts, graphs, and maps. It plays a vital role in Data Science by helping to understand trends, patterns, and outliers in data. Visualization tools like Tableau, Power BI, and Matplotlib enable data scientists to communicate complex results effectively to stakeholders. It also aids in exploratory data analysis and guides model selection. Good visualizations can reveal insights that may not be evident in raw data, making them essential for both technical analysis and business decision-making.

19. What is Python and why is it popular in Data Science?
Answer: Python is a high-level, general-purpose programming language known for its simplicity and versatility. In Data Science, Python is widely used because of its rich ecosystem of libraries like Pandas, NumPy, Scikit-learn, TensorFlow, and Matplotlib. These libraries support data manipulation, statistical analysis, machine learning, and visualization. Python's readability and community support make it accessible to beginners and powerful for experts. It also integrates easily with other technologies and platforms, making it the preferred language for data scientists, researchers, and machine learning engineers.

20. What is R and how is it used in Data Science?
Answer: R is a programming language and environment specifically designed for statistical computing and graphics. It is extensively used in Data Science for data analysis, visualization, and building statistical models. R offers a wide range of packages like ggplot2, dplyr, and caret that simplify complex analytical tasks. It is favored in academic and research settings due to its strong statistical capabilities and extensive documentation. R supports both exploratory data analysis and formal modeling, making it an essential tool for statisticians, data scientists, and analysts who focus on data interpretation and hypothesis testing.

21. What is a neural network in machine learning?
Answer: A neural network is a machine learning model inspired by the human brain's structure and function. It consists of layers of interconnected nodes (neurons) that process input data and learn complex relationships. Neural networks are the foundation of deep learning and are particularly effective for tasks like image recognition, natural language processing, and speech synthesis. Key components include input layers, hidden layers, and output layers, with each connection having weights and activation functions. Neural networks can model non-linear patterns and are highly scalable, making them suitable for large and complex datasets.

22. What is overfitting in machine learning?
Answer: Overfitting occurs when a machine learning model performs exceptionally well on training data but fails to generalize to unseen data. This happens when the model learns noise and random fluctuations instead of the underlying patterns. Overfitting leads to high variance and poor predictive performance. It can be mitigated using techniques such as cross-validation, regularization (e.g., L1, L2), pruning, or simplifying the model. Detecting overfitting is crucial for building robust models that can make accurate predictions on real-world data. Proper data splitting and monitoring performance on test data help identify overfitting early.

23. What is underfitting in machine learning?
Answer: Underfitting occurs when a machine learning model is too simple to capture the underlying structure of the data, resulting in poor performance on both training and testing datasets. This typically happens when the model lacks complexity or when features are insufficient or poorly selected. Underfitting leads to high bias and inaccurate predictions. To overcome it, one can use more complex algorithms, add more relevant features, or reduce data preprocessing that may have stripped essential patterns. Balancing model complexity and generalization is key to preventing underfitting and achieving better performance.

24. What is cross-validation in model evaluation?
Answer: ross-validation is a technique used to assess the generalization ability of a machine learning model. It involves splitting the dataset into multiple subsets or folds, training the model on some subsets, and testing it on the remaining ones. The most common type is k-fold cross-validation, where the dataset is divided into k equal parts. Cross-validation helps detect overfitting and underfitting, providing a more accurate estimate of model performance. It is widely used in model selection and hyperparameter tuning to ensure the chosen model performs well on unseen data.

25. What is a confusion matrix in classification problems?
Answer: A confusion matrix is a performance evaluation tool for classification models. It summarizes the results of predictions by displaying the counts of true positives, true negatives, false positives, and false negatives. These metrics help calculate evaluation scores like accuracy, precision, recall, and F1-score. A confusion matrix provides deeper insight than accuracy alone, especially in imbalanced datasets. For example, in a medical diagnosis scenario, identifying false negatives is crucial. Thus, using a confusion matrix allows data scientists to interpret model errors and adjust algorithms for better classification performance.

26. What is the difference between structured, semi-structured, and unstructured data?
Answer: Structured data refers to data that is organized in a defined format, typically within rows and columns of relational databases, making it easily searchable. Semi-structured data does not reside in traditional databases but still contains tags or markers (like XML or JSON) that make it easier to analyze than unstructured data. Unstructured data lacks any predefined structure and includes text, images, videos, and social media posts. Managing these types of data requires different approaches in data science and big data analytics, especially when using tools like Hadoop or Spark.

27. What is Hadoop Distributed File System (HDFS)?
Answer: HDFS is the primary storage system of the Hadoop ecosystem, designed to store and manage large datasets across multiple machines. It follows a master-slave architecture, where the NameNode manages metadata and the DataNodes store the actual data blocks. HDFS offers high fault tolerance, scalability, and data replication, typically storing three copies of each block on different nodes to ensure data reliability. It is optimized for large files and batch processing, making it a critical component in big data solutions.

28. What is a Data Lake and how is it different from a Data Warehouse?
Answer: A Data Lake is a centralized repository that allows you to store all structured, semi-structured, and

unstructured data at any scale, typically in its raw format. A Data Warehouse, on the other hand, stores data that is already cleaned and structured for specific querying and reporting purposes. Data Lakes are ideal for big data analytics and machine learning, while Data Warehouses are used for business intelligence. The flexibility of schema-on-read makes Data Lakes more adaptable, whereas Data Warehouses use schema-on-write.

29. What is the role of Python in Data Science?
Answer: Python is one of the most popular programming languages in data science due to its simplicity, extensive libraries, and strong community support. Libraries like NumPy, pandas, Matplotlib, scikit-learn, and TensorFlow enable data manipulation, visualization, and machine learning. Python is widely used for data preprocessing, statistical analysis, predictive modeling, and deployment of machine learning models. Its ability to integrate with big data tools and platforms such as Spark further strengthens its relevance in the data science ecosystem.

30. What is MapReduce in Hadoop?
Answer: MapReduce is a programming model used in the Hadoop framework to process large-scale data sets in parallel across a distributed cluster. It consists of two main tasks: the "Map" function processes input data and produces key-value pairs, and the "Reduce" function aggregates and summarizes these pairs. MapReduce simplifies complex data processing and is fault-tolerant by design. While powerful, it is being gradually replaced by more efficient frameworks like Apache Spark for certain tasks due to Spark's in-memory processing capabilities.

31. What is feature engineering and why is it important in Data Science?
Answer: Feature engineering is the process of selecting, transforming, and creating variables (features) from raw data to improve the performance of machine learning models. Good features help algorithms learn better patterns, leading to more accurate predictions. This process includes normalization, encoding categorical variables, handling missing values, and generating interaction terms. Feature engineering often requires domain knowledge and is considered one of the most critical and time-consuming steps in the data science pipeline.

32. What is Apache Spark and how does it differ from Hadoop MapReduce?
Answer: Apache Spark is an open-source big data processing engine that performs data analytics in memory, making it significantly faster than Hadoop MapReduce, which writes data to disk after each operation. Spark supports batch processing, real-time data streaming, machine learning, and graph computation through libraries like Spark Streaming, MLlib, and GraphX. It uses Resilient Distributed Datasets (RDDs) for fault tolerance. Spark's in-memory computation and ease of use make it a preferred tool for big data processing over traditional MapReduce.

33. What is overfitting in machine learning and how can it be avoided?
Answer: Overfitting occurs when a machine learning model learns not just the underlying pattern but also the noise in the training data, resulting in poor performance on new data. It can be avoided by using techniques such as cross-validation, regularization (like L1 or L2), pruning decision trees, and using simpler models. Gathering more training data and applying dropout in neural networks are also effective strategies. Detecting overfitting early is crucial for building generalizable models that perform well on unseen data.

34. What is a confusion matrix in classification problems?
Answer: A confusion matrix is a table used to evaluate the performance of a classification model. It summarizes the number of correct and incorrect predictions made by the model compared to the actual outcomes. The matrix includes four key terms: True Positives (TP), True Negatives (TN), False Positives (FP), and False Negatives (FN). From these, metrics like accuracy, precision, recall, and F1-score can be calculated. The confusion matrix provides deeper insight than overall accuracy, especially in imbalanced datasets.

35. What are the different types of machine learning algorithms?
Answer: Machine learning algorithms are broadly classified into three types: supervised learning, unsupervised learning, and reinforcement learning. Supervised learning uses labeled data to train models (e.g., linear regression, decision trees). Unsupervised learning finds patterns in unlabeled data (e.g., k-means clustering, PCA). Reinforcement learning involves learning through rewards and penalties based on actions taken in an environment (e.g., Q-learning). Choosing the right type depends on the problem statement, data availability, and desired outcome.

36. What is the curse of dimensionality in data science?
Answer: The curse of dimensionality refers to the problems that arise when analyzing data in high-dimensional spaces that do not occur in low-dimensional settings. As the number of features (dimensions) increases, the data becomes sparse, making it difficult for models to identify patterns or relationships. Distance metrics become less meaningful, which impacts clustering and classification accuracy. It also leads to overfitting. Techniques like dimensionality reduction (e.g., PCA) or feature selection are used to address this challenge and improve model performance.

37. What is Principal Component Analysis (PCA)?
Answer: Principal Component Analysis (PCA) is a statistical technique used to reduce the dimensionality of a dataset while retaining most of the variance present in the data. It transforms correlated variables into a set of uncorrelated variables called principal components, ranked by the amount of variance they capture. PCA is commonly used in data preprocessing for visualization, noise reduction, and improving algorithm efficiency. It is particularly useful when dealing with multicollinearity or datasets with many features.

38. What is a decision tree in machine learning?
Answer: A decision tree is a supervised learning algorithm used for classification and regression tasks. It splits the dataset into branches based on feature values, resulting in a tree-like structure where internal nodes represent tests on features, branches represent outcomes, and leaf nodes represent predictions. Decision trees are intuitive, easy to visualize, and interpret. However, they are prone to overfitting, which can be mitigated through pruning or by using ensemble methods like Random Forests.

39. What is a Random Forest?
Answer: A Random Forest is an ensemble learning method that combines multiple decision trees to improve prediction accuracy and control overfitting. It builds trees on random subsets of the data and features, and outputs the majority vote (classification) or average (regression) of the trees. Random Forests are robust, handle large datasets well, and can manage missing data. They are widely used due to their high accuracy and ability to model complex relationships without significant parameter tuning.

40. What is cross-validation in machine learning?
Answer: Cross-validation is a statistical technique used to assess the generalization ability of machine learning models. It involves partitioning the dataset into subsets, training the model on some subsets (training set), and validating it on the remaining (validation set). The most common form is k-fold cross-validation. It helps detect overfitting, provides a more accurate estimate of model performance, and is useful for hyperparameter tuning. Cross-validation ensures models perform well on unseen data.

41. What is a neural network?
Answer: A neural network is a machine learning model inspired by the structure of the human brain, composed of layers of interconnected nodes (neurons). Each node processes inputs using a weighted sum and an activation function. Neural networks are capable of learning complex patterns in data and are widely used in image recognition, natural language processing, and predictive analytics. Deep neural networks, with many hidden layers, form the foundation of deep learning.

42. What is the role of activation functions in neural networks?
Answer: Activation functions determine whether a neuron should be activated or not by transforming the weighted input into an output signal. They introduce non-linearity into the model, allowing neural networks to learn complex patterns. Common activation functions include Sigmoid, Tanh, and ReLU (Rectified Linear Unit). The choice of activation function affects the network's learning efficiency and ability to converge. Without activation functions, a neural network would behave like a linear model.

43. What is deep learning and how does it relate to big data?
Answer: Deep learning is a subset of machine learning that uses neural networks with multiple layers (deep neural networks) to model high-level abstractions in data. It is particularly effective for tasks involving unstructured data like images, audio, and text. Deep learning requires large amounts of data and computational power, making it highly suitable for big data environments. It plays a key role in applications such as autonomous vehicles, medical imaging, and voice assistants.

44. What is clustering in unsupervised learning?
Answer: Clustering is a technique in unsupervised learning used to group similar data points together based on their features without labeled output. It helps in discovering hidden patterns and data segmentation. Popular clustering algorithms include k-means, hierarchical clustering, and DBSCAN. Clustering is used in customer segmentation, image compression, market basket analysis, and anomaly detection. It requires selecting the right number of clusters and appropriate distance measures for meaningful insights.

45. What is k-means clustering and how does it work?
Answer: K-means is a popular clustering algorithm that partitions data into k distinct clusters based on feature similarity. It works by initializing k centroids, assigning each data point to the nearest centroid, then recalculating centroids based on the assigned points. This process repeats until the centroids stabilize. K-means is efficient but sensitive to initial centroid placement and the value of k. It assumes spherical clusters and equal variance, which may not suit all datasets.

46. What is natural language processing (NLP)?
Answer: Natural Language Processing (NLP) is a field of artificial intelligence that enables machines to understand, interpret, and generate human language. It combines linguistics, computer science, and machine learning. Applications include sentiment analysis, language translation, chatbots, and text summarization. NLP techniques involve tokenization, stemming, named entity recognition, and part-of-speech tagging. With the advent of big data and deep learning, NLP has achieved significant advancements, such as using transformers and models like BERT and GPT.

47. What is sentiment analysis?
Answer: Sentiment analysis is an NLP technique used to determine the emotional tone behind a body of text. It classifies text as positive, negative, or neutral, providing insights into public opinion, customer feedback, and social media sentiments. It uses techniques like machine learning, lexicon-based approaches, or deep learning. Sentiment analysis helps businesses improve customer satisfaction, monitor brand reputation, and make data-driven decisions based on consumer sentiment.

48. What is anomaly detection in data science?
Answer: Anomaly detection involves identifying data points that deviate significantly from the norm. These outliers can indicate critical incidents like fraud, equipment failures, or security breaches. Techniques include statistical methods, clustering, and machine learning algorithms such as isolation forests and autoencoders. Anomaly detection is widely used in finance, healthcare, cybersecurity, and industrial monitoring. It enhances operational efficiency and risk mitigation by enabling early warning systems and real-time alerts.

49. What is data wrangling?
Answer: Data wrangling, also known as data munging, is the process of cleaning, transforming, and organizing raw data into a usable format for analysis. It includes handling missing values, correcting data types, removing duplicates, and reshaping datasets. Data wrangling is a critical step in the data science workflow because high-quality input data leads to better model performance. Tools like Python (pandas), R, and Power Query are commonly used for data wrangling tasks.

50. What is a recommendation system?
Answer: A recommendation system is an algorithm that suggests items to users based on preferences, behaviors, or past interactions. It is widely used in e-commerce, streaming platforms, and online services. There are mainly three types: content-based filtering, collaborative filtering, and hybrid systems. These systems improve user engagement, retention, and sales. Machine learning and big data play a central role in building scalable and accurate recommendation engines by processing massive amounts of user data in real time.

51. What is feature engineering in data science?
Answer: Feature engineering is the process of creating new input features or modifying existing ones to improve the performance of machine learning models. It involves selecting relevant features, transforming variables, encoding categorical data, handling missing values, and creating interaction terms. Effective feature engineering enhances model accuracy, reduces complexity, and enables algorithms to extract meaningful patterns. It combines domain knowledge with data insights and is often considered more crucial than choosing the model itself.

52. What is the difference between batch processing and stream processing in big data?
Answer: Batch processing involves collecting, storing, and processing large volumes of data at once, typically at scheduled intervals. Stream processing, on the other hand, analyzes data in real-time as it is generated. Batch processing is suitable for historical analysis and reporting, while stream processing is ideal for real-time applications like fraud detection or live analytics. Technologies like Hadoop support batch processing, whereas Apache Kafka and Apache Flink enable stream processing.

53. What is Apache Spark?
Answer: Apache Spark is an open-source, distributed computing system used for big data processing. It provides fast in-memory data processing and supports batch and stream processing, machine learning, and graph analytics. Spark's core component is the Resilient Distributed Dataset (RDD), which allows fault-tolerant, parallel data operations. It is widely adopted for its speed, scalability, and ability to work with large datasets. Spark integrates well with Hadoop, HDFS, and other big data tools.

54. What is Apache Hadoop and its components?
Answer: Apache Hadoop is an open-source framework for distributed storage and processing of large datasets across clusters of computers. Its core components include HDFS (Hadoop Distributed File System) for data storage, MapReduce for data processing, YARN for resource management, and Hadoop Common for utilities. Hadoop allows organizations to handle vast volumes of data efficiently and is foundational in many big data ecosystems.

55. What is data normalization and why is it important?
Answer: Data normalization is a preprocessing technique used to scale numerical values to a common range, often between 0 and 1. It helps ensure that all features contribute equally to the model, especially in algorithms sensitive to the magnitude of data like KNN or neural networks. Normalization improves convergence in gradient-based models and enhances performance. Common methods include Min-Max Scaling and Z-score normalization.

56. What is data standardization?
Answer: Data standardization involves rescaling data to have a mean of 0 and a standard deviation of 1. It is particularly useful when features have different units or scales. Standardization ensures that data conforms to a normal distribution, making it suitable for algorithms like logistic regression, SVM, and PCA. It helps models learn more effectively and improves interpretability and comparability of features.

57. What is an ROC curve in classification models?
Answer: The Receiver Operating Characteristic (ROC) curve is a graphical representation of a classification model's performance across all classification thresholds. It plots the True Positive Rate (Sensitivity) against the False Positive Rate (1 – Specificity). The Area Under the Curve (AUC) measures model accuracy; a value closer to 1 indicates better performance. ROC curves help compare different classifiers and evaluate trade-offs between sensitivity and specificity.

58. What is overfitting in machine learning?
Answer: Overfitting occurs when a machine learning model learns the noise and random fluctuations in the training data rather than the underlying patterns. As a result, it performs well on training data but poorly on unseen data. Overfitting can be caused by overly complex models, too many features, or insufficient training data. Solutions include using regularization, pruning, cross-validation, and simplifying the model.

59. What is underfitting in machine learning?
Answer: Underfitting happens when a model is too simple to capture the underlying structure of the data, resulting in poor performance on both training and test datasets. It fails to learn from the data and generalizes poorly. Causes of underfitting include insufficient features, overly simplistic models, or inadequate training. Increasing model complexity, adding features, or using more advanced algorithms can help overcome underfitting.

60. What is a confusion matrix?
Answer: A confusion matrix is a performance measurement tool for classification models. It displays the counts of true positives, true negatives, false positives, and false negatives. This matrix helps compute various metrics like

accuracy, precision, recall, and F1-score. It provides a comprehensive view of the model's predictive performance and is essential for identifying types of classification errors.

61. What is BigQuery and how is it used in data science?
Answer: Google BigQuery is a fully-managed, serverless data warehouse that allows scalable and fast SQL-based analytics on large datasets. It is used in data science for querying big data, building dashboards, and running machine learning models directly on structured data. BigQuery supports integration with Google Cloud's AI tools, provides real-time data processing, and is ideal for interactive analysis with massive datasets.

62. What is the difference between structured, semi-structured, and unstructured data?
Answer: Structured data resides in fixed fields within databases, such as tables with rows and columns. Semi-structured data does not follow a rigid schema but contains tags or markers, like JSON or XML. Unstructured data lacks a predefined format and includes images, videos, text, and audio. Data science and big data tools are designed to extract insights from all three types, using databases, NoSQL systems, and natural language processing.

63. What is map-reduce in big data?
Answer: MapReduce is a programming model used for processing large datasets in a distributed environment. The "Map" step transforms input data into key-value pairs, and the "Reduce" step aggregates or summarizes the results. Originally developed by Google and implemented in Hadoop, MapReduce is efficient for tasks like sorting, filtering, and summarizing data. It enables parallel processing across clusters and handles faults automatically.

64. What is data sampling and why is it used?
Answer: Data sampling involves selecting a subset of data from a larger dataset for analysis. It is used to reduce computational costs, speed up model training, and enable faster experimentation. Sampling must preserve the characteristics of the full dataset to ensure model accuracy. Common techniques include random sampling, stratified sampling, and systematic sampling. Proper sampling supports scalable data science workflows.

65. What is text mining in data science?
Answer: Text mining, or text analytics, is the process of extracting meaningful information from unstructured text data. It involves techniques like keyword extraction, sentiment analysis, topic modeling, and text classification. Text mining is used in applications like customer feedback analysis, social media monitoring, and document summarization. It combines natural language processing, statistical analysis, and machine learning to transform text into actionable insights.

66. What is Hadoop Distributed File System (HDFS)?
Answer: HDFS is the primary storage system of the Hadoop framework. It stores large files across multiple machines in a distributed fashion, ensuring fault tolerance and scalability. Files are split into blocks and replicated across nodes for redundancy. HDFS supports high-throughput data access and is optimized for batch processing. It enables efficient storage and retrieval of big data in a cluster environment.

67. What is the use of Python in data science?
Answer: Python is a widely used programming language in data science due to its simplicity, readability, and vast library ecosystem. Libraries like NumPy, Pandas, Matplotlib, Scikit-learn, and TensorFlow support data analysis, visualization, machine learning, and deep learning. Python's versatility makes it suitable for data wrangling, exploratory analysis, model building, and deployment. It is preferred for both academic and industry applications.

68. What is data skew and how does it affect big data processing?
Answer: Data skew occurs when data is unevenly distributed across partitions in a distributed system, causing some nodes to handle more data than others. This leads to performance bottlenecks and inefficient processing. In big data platforms like Hadoop or Spark, data skew can result in task delays and resource imbalance. Solutions include repartitioning, data balancing, and optimizing algorithms to handle skewed data.

69. What is data versioning?
Answer: Data versioning is the practice of maintaining different versions of datasets to track changes, ensure reproducibility, and support collaborative workflows. It allows data scientists to revert to previous versions, compare

results, and audit data evolution. Tools like DVC (Data Version Control) and Delta Lake provide data versioning capabilities. It is crucial in machine learning pipelines where both data and models evolve over time.

70. What is data lineage and why is it important?
Answer: Data lineage refers to the tracking of data's origin, transformations, and movement throughout its lifecycle. It provides visibility into how data flows from source to destination, ensuring transparency and accountability. Data lineage helps in debugging data issues, regulatory compliance, and impact analysis. It is vital in data governance frameworks and supports trust in data-driven decision-making processes.

71. What is the role of data governance in data science?
Answer: Data governance refers to the framework and practices that ensure data integrity, security, quality, and usability across an organization. In data science, data governance is essential for maintaining trustworthy and accurate data, complying with regulatory requirements, and promoting responsible data use. It defines roles, responsibilities, and policies for data access and management. Effective governance ensures that data is reliable, consistent, and suitable for analysis, which enhances decision-making and model performance.

72. What is Apache Hive used for in big data processing?
Answer: Apache Hive is a data warehouse infrastructure built on top of Hadoop that allows users to query and manage large datasets using a SQL-like language called HiveQL. It is designed for batch processing and is ideal for users familiar with SQL but less with Java or MapReduce. Hive translates queries into MapReduce jobs, enabling efficient data summarization, querying, and analysis on large datasets stored in HDFS or similar systems.

73. What is a recommendation system?
Answer: A recommendation system is a machine learning-based tool used to suggest products, services, or information to users based on their preferences and behavior. These systems use algorithms such as collaborative filtering, content-based filtering, or hybrid approaches. Recommendation systems are widely used in e-commerce, entertainment platforms, and social media. They enhance user experience by personalizing content and increasing engagement and sales.

74. What is an ensemble learning technique in machine learning?
Answer: Ensemble learning combines multiple models to produce better predictive performance than any single model. It can be done using methods like bagging, boosting, and stacking. Techniques such as Random Forest (bagging) and Gradient Boosting Machines (boosting) reduce variance and bias, respectively. Ensemble models are robust, less prone to overfitting, and often used in high-performing data science competitions and production systems.

75. What is the use of NoSQL databases in big data?
Answer: NoSQL databases are non-relational databases designed to handle large volumes of unstructured or semi-structured data. They provide scalability, flexibility, and high performance, making them suitable for big data applications. Common types include document databases (MongoDB), column-family stores (Cassandra), key-value stores (Redis), and graph databases (Neo4j). NoSQL databases support real-time processing and are widely used in applications involving large-scale user data and content.

76. What is sentiment analysis in data science?
Answer: Sentiment analysis is a natural language processing technique used to determine the emotional tone or sentiment expressed in text. It classifies text as positive, negative, or neutral. This technique is commonly applied to customer feedback, social media posts, and product reviews to gauge public opinion. Sentiment analysis helps businesses understand customer emotions, monitor brand reputation, and improve service.

77. What is PCA (Principal Component Analysis)?
Answer: Principal Component Analysis (PCA) is a dimensionality reduction technique used to reduce the number of variables in a dataset while preserving as much variance as possible. It transforms the original features into a new set of uncorrelated variables called principal components. PCA helps in visualizing high-dimensional data, improving model performance, and eliminating multicollinearity. It is especially useful in preprocessing before applying machine learning models.

78. What is a data lake?
Answer: A data lake is a centralized repository that stores vast amounts of raw data in its native format, including structured, semi-structured, and unstructured data. Unlike traditional databases, data lakes do not require predefined schemas, allowing for flexible data ingestion. They support advanced analytics, machine learning, and real-time processing. Technologies like AWS S3, Azure Data Lake, and Hadoop-based systems are commonly used to build data lakes.

79. What is A/B testing in data science?
Answer: A/B testing is a statistical method used to compare two versions of a variable (A and B) to determine which one performs better. It is widely used in marketing, web design, and product development to optimize user experience and decision-making. The test involves randomly assigning users to either version and analyzing differences in outcomes like click-through rates or conversions. It supports data-driven decisions and minimizes risks.

80. What is data anonymization and why is it important?
Answer: Data anonymization is the process of protecting personal or sensitive information by modifying or removing identifiable data elements. It ensures that individuals cannot be traced back using the available data. Anonymization techniques include masking, generalization, and data perturbation. It is essential for complying with privacy regulations like GDPR and HIPAA and enables data scientists to work with real-world datasets without compromising user privacy.

81. What is model deployment in data science?
Answer: Model deployment is the process of integrating a trained machine learning model into a production environment so that it can make real-time predictions or decisions. It involves packaging the model, building APIs, monitoring performance, and ensuring scalability. Tools like Flask, FastAPI, Docker, and cloud platforms such as AWS, Azure, and GCP are commonly used. Effective deployment bridges the gap between data science and business use cases.

82. What is a data pipeline?
Answer: A data pipeline is a series of processes that automate the movement, transformation, and storage of data from source to destination. It may include steps such as data extraction, cleansing, enrichment, and loading into data warehouses or lakes. Data pipelines are essential for maintaining consistent, timely, and accurate data flows, and they support both batch and real-time data processing. Tools like Apache NiFi, Airflow, and Talend are commonly used.

83. What is the difference between classification and regression in machine learning?
Answer: Classification is a supervised learning task that predicts categorical labels (e.g., spam or not spam), while regression predicts continuous numerical values (e.g., house price). Algorithms like decision trees, logistic regression, and SVM are used for classification, whereas linear regression and random forest regressors are used for regression. Choosing between them depends on the nature of the target variable.

84. What is the curse of dimensionality in data science?
Answer: The curse of dimensionality refers to the problems that arise when working with high-dimensional data. As the number of features increases, the volume of the feature space grows exponentially, making data sparse and patterns harder to identify. It affects model performance, increases computation time, and may lead to overfitting. Dimensionality reduction techniques like PCA and feature selection help mitigate these issues.

85. What is time series analysis?
Answer: Time series analysis involves analyzing data points collected or recorded at specific time intervals to understand trends, seasonality, and cyclic behavior. It is widely used in financial forecasting, demand prediction, and weather modeling. Techniques include ARIMA, exponential smoothing, and seasonal decomposition. Time series models differ from others because they account for the temporal ordering and dependencies within data.

86. What is the difference between SQL and NoSQL databases?
Answer: SQL databases are relational and use structured schemas, supporting complex queries through SQL. They ensure ACID properties and are ideal for structured data. NoSQL databases are non-relational, schema-less, and support flexible data models, making them suitable for unstructured or semi-structured data. SQL databases include

MySQL and PostgreSQL, while NoSQL includes MongoDB, Cassandra, and Redis. The choice depends on data type, scalability needs, and consistency requirements.

87. What is model drift and how is it handled?
Answer: Model drift occurs when a machine learning model's performance degrades over time due to changes in data patterns. This can be due to concept drift, where the relationship between inputs and outputs changes, or data drift, where the input distribution shifts. Handling model drift involves regular monitoring, retraining with updated data, and using adaptive models. Detecting drift is crucial for maintaining model accuracy in production.

88. What is the use of Apache Kafka in data science?
Answer: Apache Kafka is a distributed streaming platform used for building real-time data pipelines and applications. It enables high-throughput, fault-tolerant, and scalable data ingestion and processing. In data science, Kafka is used to collect and stream large volumes of data from multiple sources to downstream systems like data lakes, processing engines, or ML models. It supports event-driven architectures and real-time analytics.

89. What is a heatmap in data visualization?
Answer: A heatmap is a graphical representation of data where individual values are represented as colors. It is used to show the magnitude of a phenomenon across two dimensions and is useful for correlation matrices, feature importance, and activity tracking. Heatmaps help identify patterns, trends, and outliers in datasets and are commonly used in exploratory data analysis. Tools like Seaborn and Matplotlib in Python are used to create heatmaps.

90. What is tokenization in natural language processing?
Answer: Tokenization is the process of breaking text into smaller units called tokens, such as words, phrases, or characters. It is a fundamental step in NLP for preparing text data for analysis or model input. Tokenization enables operations like stop-word removal, stemming, and vectorization. Libraries like NLTK, SpaCy, and transformers use efficient tokenizers to process large text corpora in various languages.

91. What is a confusion matrix in machine learning?
Answer: A confusion matrix is a performance measurement tool used for evaluating classification models. It displays the number of true positives, true negatives, false positives, and false negatives. From this matrix, important metrics like accuracy, precision, recall, and F1-score can be derived. It provides a more comprehensive understanding of a model's prediction capability beyond just overall accuracy.

92. What is the purpose of normalization in data preprocessing?
Answer: Normalization transforms data to a common scale without distorting differences in the ranges of values. It is particularly important for algorithms like k-nearest neighbors and neural networks, which are sensitive to feature scaling. Techniques such as Min-Max normalization and Z-score standardization help improve model convergence and ensure fair treatment of features during training.

93. What is the role of APIs in deploying data science models?
Answer: APIs (Application Programming Interfaces) enable interaction between a deployed model and other software systems. By creating RESTful APIs using frameworks like Flask or FastAPI, data scientists can expose their models to be consumed by web apps, mobile apps, or enterprise systems. APIs make it easier to integrate machine learning models into real-time production environments.

94. What are hyperparameters in machine learning?
Answer: Hyperparameters are configuration settings used to control the learning process of a machine learning algorithm. Unlike model parameters, which are learned from the data, hyperparameters are set prior to training. Examples include learning rate, number of trees in a random forest, and regularization strength. Tuning these values can significantly affect model performance.

95. What is the ROC curve?
Answer: The Receiver Operating Characteristic (ROC) curve is a graphical plot that illustrates the performance of a binary classification model at various threshold settings. It plots the True Positive Rate (TPR) against the False Positive Rate (FPR). The area under the curve (AUC) provides a single metric to evaluate model performance — the closer to 1, the better the model.

96. What is the function of Hadoop in big data?
Answer: Hadoop is an open-source framework that allows distributed storage and processing of large datasets using clusters of computers. Its core components include HDFS for storage and MapReduce for computation. Hadoop is fault-tolerant, scalable, and cost-effective, making it ideal for handling big data workloads across industries.

97. What is clustering in unsupervised learning?
Answer: Clustering is an unsupervised learning technique used to group similar data points based on features without predefined labels. Algorithms like K-means, DBSCAN, and hierarchical clustering identify natural groupings within data. Clustering is used in market segmentation, anomaly detection, and image compression, among other applications.

98. What is big data analytics?
Answer: Big data analytics refers to the process of examining large and varied data sets — both structured and unstructured — to uncover hidden patterns, unknown correlations, market trends, and customer preferences. Tools and technologies like Hadoop, Spark, and NoSQL databases help perform real-time, predictive, and prescriptive analytics at scale.

99. What is deep learning?
Answer: Deep learning is a subset of machine learning that uses neural networks with many layers (deep neural networks) to model complex patterns in data. It excels at tasks such as image and speech recognition, natural language processing, and autonomous systems. Frameworks like TensorFlow and PyTorch are widely used for developing deep learning models.

100. What is feature selection in data science?
Answer: Feature selection is the process of choosing the most relevant input variables for model training. It helps reduce dimensionality, improves model accuracy, and reduces overfitting. Methods include filter-based (e.g., correlation), wrapper-based (e.g., recursive feature elimination), and embedded techniques (e.g., Lasso). Proper feature selection enhances both model interpretability and performance.

101. What is ensemble learning in machine learning?
Answer: Ensemble learning is a machine learning technique that combines predictions from multiple models to improve accuracy and robustness over individual models. Common ensemble methods include bagging, boosting, and stacking. For example, Random Forest uses bagging to build multiple decision trees, while AdaBoost applies boosting to correct the errors of weak learners. Ensemble methods reduce variance, bias, and help mitigate overfitting. By leveraging the strengths of different models, ensemble learning often outperforms single-model approaches and is widely used in real-world applications like fraud detection, recommendation systems, and financial forecasting.

102. What is MapReduce in big data?
Answer: MapReduce is a programming model used in big data processing to perform parallel computation over large datasets. It consists of two main functions: the Map function processes input data into intermediate key-value pairs, and the Reduce function aggregates those pairs into final results. MapReduce runs on distributed systems like Hadoop and provides fault tolerance, scalability, and simplicity for batch processing tasks. It is useful for operations like filtering, counting, sorting, and summarizing large volumes of data, and it enables organizations to analyze big data efficiently across multiple servers.

103. What is the difference between ETL and ELT?
Answer: ETL (Extract, Transform, Load) and ELT (Extract, Load, Transform) are two data integration methods. In ETL, data is extracted from sources, transformed into a suitable format, and then loaded into the target database. In contrast, ELT first extracts and loads raw data into the target system (like a data lake), where transformation occurs afterward using the system's processing power. ETL is traditional and used with data warehouses, while ELT is preferred for modern big data platforms. ELT supports large-scale unstructured data and allows greater flexibility in data processing.

104. What is dimensionality reduction in data science?
Answer: Dimensionality reduction is the process of reducing the number of input variables or features in a dataset. It helps eliminate irrelevant or redundant features, enhances model performance, reduces overfitting, and improves

visualization. Common techniques include Principal Component Analysis (PCA) and t-Distributed Stochastic Neighbor Embedding (t-SNE). These techniques transform high-dimensional data into fewer dimensions while preserving important information. Dimensionality reduction is crucial in handling datasets with hundreds or thousands of features, especially in image processing, text mining, and genomics.

105. What is NoSQL and how does it differ from SQL databases?
Answer: NoSQL databases are designed to handle large volumes of unstructured or semi-structured data, offering high scalability and flexibility. Unlike SQL databases, which store data in tables with predefined schemas, NoSQL databases use various data models like key-value, document, column-family, and graph formats. They are schema-less, horizontally scalable, and well-suited for big data and real-time web applications. Examples include MongoDB (document), Cassandra (column), and Redis (key-value). NoSQL systems prioritize performance and availability, making them ideal for IoT, social media, and content management systems.

106. What is feature engineering in machine learning?
Answer: Feature engineering is the process of creating, transforming, or selecting input variables to improve the performance of machine learning models. It involves techniques such as handling missing values, encoding categorical variables, creating new interaction terms, or applying domain knowledge to derive more informative features. Proper feature engineering often leads to better model accuracy and generalization. It is considered one of the most critical steps in the data science workflow, as well-engineered features can sometimes outperform more complex algorithms.

107. What is Spark Streaming?
Answer: Spark Streaming is a component of Apache Spark that enables real-time data processing. It ingests live data streams from sources like Kafka, Flume, or TCP sockets, processes them using Spark's core engine, and outputs the results to data storage or dashboards. Unlike batch processing, Spark Streaming works on micro-batches and allows scalable, high-throughput, and fault-tolerant stream processing. It is used in use-cases like fraud detection, monitoring, real-time analytics, and alerting systems. Spark Streaming integrates seamlessly with Spark's ecosystem, making it ideal for unified batch and stream processing.

108. What is the importance of metadata in big data?
Answer: Metadata is data that describes other data. In big data systems, metadata provides crucial context about datasets—such as source, format, owner, creation date, and structure. It enables data discovery, classification, and efficient data management. Metadata helps in understanding data lineage, ensuring data governance, and maintaining data quality. Without proper metadata, managing large and complex datasets becomes difficult. Tools like Apache Atlas and Informatica are used to handle metadata in big data ecosystems, aiding compliance, auditing, and data cataloging processes.

109. What is the role of data visualization in data science?
Answer: Data visualization helps transform raw data into meaningful graphical representations like charts, graphs, and dashboards. It enables data scientists and stakeholders to identify trends, patterns, and anomalies more effectively than raw numbers. Visualization tools like Tableau, Power BI, and matplotlib facilitate interactive exploration and communication of insights. Good visualizations enhance decision-making, storytelling, and the interpretability of complex models. They also bridge the gap between technical teams and non-technical stakeholders, making data insights more accessible and actionable.

110. What is a recommendation system in data science?
Answer: A recommendation system is a machine learning-based approach that predicts user preferences and suggests relevant items. It is widely used in e-commerce, streaming services, and social media platforms. There are three main types: collaborative filtering (based on user-item interactions), content-based filtering (based on item features), and hybrid approaches (combining both). These systems analyze historical behavior, preferences, and ratings to generate personalized recommendations. They enhance user experience, increase engagement, and drive revenue by helping users discover content or products of interest.

111. What is overfitting in machine learning?
Answer: Overfitting occurs when a machine learning model learns the training data too well, capturing noise or irrelevant patterns, and performs poorly on unseen data. This results in high accuracy on training data but low generalization to test data. Overfitting can be caused by overly complex models, insufficient data, or lack of

regularization. Techniques like cross-validation, pruning, dropout, and regularization methods (L1/L2) are used to prevent overfitting. Addressing overfitting is crucial for building reliable and robust predictive models.

112. What is underfitting in machine learning?
Answer: Underfitting happens when a machine learning model is too simple to capture the underlying patterns in the data, leading to poor performance on both training and testing sets. It usually results from choosing models with too few parameters or insufficient training. Underfitting indicates that the model has high bias and fails to represent the complexity of the data. Solutions include increasing model complexity, adding more features, reducing bias, or using better feature engineering. Balancing model bias and variance is key to achieving optimal performance.

113. What is data wrangling?
Answer: Data wrangling, also known as data munging, refers to the process of cleaning, structuring, and enriching raw data into a format suitable for analysis. It includes tasks such as handling missing values, correcting data types, filtering out noise, and normalizing formats. Effective data wrangling ensures data quality and reliability, which are essential for accurate insights and model building. Tools like Python's pandas, R's dplyr, and platforms like Trifacta support data wrangling. It is a crucial step that typically consumes the majority of a data scientist's time.

114. What is cross-validation in machine learning?
Answer: Cross-validation is a technique used to assess the performance and generalizability of a machine learning model by splitting the dataset into multiple training and testing subsets. The most common form is k-fold cross-validation, where the data is divided into k parts; each part is used as a test set once while the rest serve as training data. This process reduces the risk of overfitting and provides a more accurate estimate of model performance on unseen data. It is a standard best practice in model evaluation.

115. What is the difference between batch and real-time data processing?
Answer: Batch processing involves collecting and storing large volumes of data over time and processing it in bulk, usually during off-peak hours. It is suitable for tasks like reporting, backups, and billing. Real-time processing, on the other hand, analyzes data instantly as it arrives, enabling immediate responses. It is ideal for applications like fraud detection, live monitoring, and streaming analytics. Tools like Apache Hadoop are used for batch processing, while Apache Kafka and Apache Spark handle real-time streams. The choice depends on latency requirements and data volume.

116. What is a neural network?
Answer: A neural network is a machine learning model inspired by the structure of the human brain. It consists of interconnected layers of nodes (neurons), where each node processes inputs using activation functions and passes the result to the next layer. Neural networks are used for complex tasks such as image recognition, language translation, and autonomous driving. Types include feedforward, convolutional (CNNs), and recurrent neural networks (RNNs). They learn patterns from data through backpropagation and are the foundation of deep learning models.

117. What is a data pipeline?
Answer: A data pipeline is a series of processes that automate the movement and transformation of data from source systems to target destinations, such as databases or data warehouses. It involves steps like data extraction, transformation, loading (ETL), validation, and storage. Data pipelines ensure data is delivered consistently, efficiently, and in the right format for analysis. Tools like Apache NiFi, Airflow, and AWS Data Pipeline are commonly used. Building robust data pipelines is critical in big data and real-time analytics environments.

118. What is anomaly detection?
Answer: Anomaly detection involves identifying data points that deviate significantly from the normal pattern. These outliers can indicate errors, fraud, system failures, or unusual behavior. Techniques include statistical methods, clustering, and machine learning models such as isolation forests or autoencoders. Anomaly detection is widely used in cybersecurity, quality control, healthcare, and finance. Detecting anomalies early helps prevent costly issues and supports risk management.

119. What is the importance of data governance in data science?
Answer: Data governance refers to the policies, procedures, and standards that ensure the effective and secure management of data within an organization. It ensures data accuracy, consistency, privacy, and compliance with

regulations like GDPR or HIPAA. In data science, governance supports data quality, lineage, and accountability. It enables trusted decision-making, reduces risk, and aligns data initiatives with business goals. Strong data governance is essential for maintaining credibility, especially when data is used for critical analytics and AI applications.

120. What is the Internet of Behaviors (IoB)?
Answer: The Internet of Behaviors (IoB) extends the Internet of Things by capturing and analyzing data about user behavior through connected devices. IoB leverages data from wearable tech, smartphones, smart home devices, and online activity to influence or understand user actions. It is used in areas like personalized marketing, health monitoring, and customer service optimization. While powerful, IoB raises ethical concerns regarding privacy and data security. Its integration with big data and AI enables behavior-based predictions and interventions.

121. What is batch normalization in deep learning?
Answer: Batch normalization is a technique to improve the training of deep neural networks by normalizing the input of each layer to have zero mean and unit variance. It helps accelerate training, reduce sensitivity to initialization, and combat internal covariate shift. By stabilizing the learning process, batch normalization enables deeper networks to converge faster and more reliably. It is widely used in convolutional and fully connected layers of deep learning architectures.

122. What is LSTM and how is it used in time series data?
Answer: LSTM (Long Short-Term Memory) is a type of recurrent neural network (RNN) designed to model long-term dependencies in sequential data. It overcomes the vanishing gradient problem in traditional RNNs by using memory cells and gating mechanisms. LSTMs are particularly effective in time series forecasting, natural language processing, and speech recognition. They learn from sequences of data, capturing trends and patterns over time, making them ideal for applications like stock prediction or weather forecasting.

123. What is reinforcement learning and its applications?
Answer: Reinforcement learning is a machine learning paradigm where an agent learns to make decisions by interacting with an environment and receiving feedback in the form of rewards or penalties. The goal is to maximize cumulative rewards over time. It is used in robotics, game playing (like AlphaGo), self-driving cars, and personalized recommendations. Reinforcement learning involves exploration-exploitation trade-offs and uses algorithms like Q-learning and Deep Q-Networks (DQN) to learn optimal policies.

124. What is the role of feature engineering in data science?
Answer: Feature engineering is the process of creating new input variables or modifying existing ones to improve the performance of machine learning models. It involves selecting, transforming, and extracting features that capture relevant information. Good feature engineering can significantly enhance model accuracy and interpretability. Techniques include one-hot encoding, binning, normalization, and polynomial features. It is considered both an art and science, requiring domain knowledge and creativity.

125. What is federated learning and how does it ensure data privacy?
Answer: Federated learning is a decentralized machine learning approach where models are trained locally on edge devices, and only the model updates are shared with a central server, not the raw data. This ensures data privacy and security, making it suitable for sensitive applications like healthcare and mobile device personalization. It reduces the need to transmit large datasets and complies with data protection regulations. Federated learning is supported by companies like Google and Apple for privacy-preserving AI development.

Chapter 6: Most Asked Questions Part-B

1. What is the difference between Data Science and Big Data?
Answer: Data Science is a multidisciplinary field that focuses on extracting insights, patterns, and knowledge from structured and unstructured data using techniques like statistics, machine learning, and data visualization. Big Data, on the other hand, refers to extremely large data sets that traditional data processing tools cannot handle efficiently. Big Data deals more with storage, processing frameworks (like Hadoop and Spark), and data volume, velocity, and variety. While Big Data provides the infrastructure and methods to manage massive data sets, Data Science applies analytical and statistical techniques to derive value from that data.

2. What are the five V's of Big Data?
Answer: The five V's of Big Data are Volume, Velocity, Variety, Veracity, and Value. Volume refers to the massive amount of data generated every second. Velocity indicates the speed at which data is generated and processed. Variety represents the different forms of data, such as structured, semi-structured, and unstructured. Veracity is the quality and accuracy of the data, ensuring it is trustworthy. Value is about extracting meaningful insights from the data. These five characteristics define the complexity of Big Data and guide the tools and techniques used for its processing and analysis.

3. What is Hadoop and how does it relate to Big Data?
Answer: Hadoop is an open-source framework developed by Apache that allows the distributed processing of large data sets across clusters of computers using simple programming models. It is highly scalable, fault-tolerant, and designed to handle large volumes of structured and unstructured data. The core components of Hadoop include the Hadoop Distributed File System (HDFS) and MapReduce for processing. Hadoop plays a crucial role in Big Data as it allows companies to store and analyze data efficiently without needing expensive hardware. It laid the foundation for many other Big Data technologies and ecosystems.

4. What is MapReduce in Hadoop?
Answer: MapReduce is a programming model and processing technique used within the Hadoop framework to process and generate large data sets. It consists of two main functions: the Map function, which processes input data and produces key-value pairs, and the Reduce function, which aggregates or summarizes those intermediate results. MapReduce enables parallel processing by distributing the tasks across a Hadoop cluster. It is fault-tolerant and scalable, allowing complex computations to be handled efficiently. While newer tools like Spark have become more popular, MapReduce is still fundamental to understanding Hadoop's operation.

5. What is HDFS in Hadoop?
Answer: HDFS stands for Hadoop Distributed File System. It is the primary storage system used by Hadoop applications to manage large amounts of data across multiple machines in a cluster. HDFS divides data into blocks and distributes them across nodes, ensuring redundancy and fault tolerance through data replication. The system consists of a NameNode (manages metadata) and multiple DataNodes (store actual data). HDFS is optimized for high-throughput access and is best suited for batch processing rather than low-latency access. Its reliability and scalability make it an essential part of any Big Data solution.

6. What is Apache Spark and how does it improve over Hadoop MapReduce?
Answer: Apache Spark is an open-source data processing engine designed for speed and ease of use in Big Data analytics. Unlike Hadoop MapReduce, which reads and writes from disk between every operation, Spark processes data in-memory, which significantly speeds up data processing tasks. Spark supports batch processing, real-time streaming, machine learning, and graph processing within the same framework. Its APIs are available in Java, Scala, Python, and R, making it accessible to a wide range of developers. Spark improves upon Hadoop MapReduce in terms of performance, ease of development, and support for complex data workflows.

7. What is a Data Lake and how is it different from a Data Warehouse?
Answer: A Data Lake is a centralized repository that stores large amounts of raw data in its native format, including structured, semi-structured, and unstructured data. It is highly scalable and typically built on low-cost storage systems like Hadoop HDFS or cloud platforms. In contrast, a Data Warehouse stores processed, structured data optimized for

querying and analysis, often using SQL-based tools. Data Lakes support real-time analytics, machine learning, and advanced data exploration, whereas Data Warehouses are preferred for business intelligence and reporting. The key difference lies in the structure, use-case, and processing stage of the stored data.

8. What is NoSQL and why is it important in Big Data?
Answer: NoSQL refers to a class of non-relational databases designed to handle large volumes of diverse data types, including unstructured and semi-structured data. Unlike traditional relational databases, NoSQL databases are schema-less and support flexible data models such as key-value, document, column-family, and graph. They are highly scalable, distributed, and optimized for performance in Big Data environments. NoSQL databases like MongoDB, Cassandra, and HBase are essential in Big Data for real-time analytics, scalability, and managing complex and fast-changing data, especially from web applications, IoT devices, and social media.

9. What is the role of machine learning in Data Science?
Answer: Machine learning (ML) is a core component of Data Science that enables systems to learn from data and make predictions or decisions without being explicitly programmed. It involves building algorithms that can identify patterns, learn from historical data, and apply that knowledge to new data. ML is used in Data Science for tasks such as classification, regression, clustering, and anomaly detection. It powers applications like recommendation systems, fraud detection, natural language processing, and predictive maintenance. ML enhances Data Science by automating insights extraction and supporting scalable data-driven decision-making.

10. What is the significance of data lineage in Data Science projects?
Answer: Data lineage refers to the lifecycle of data as it moves through various stages—from source to destination—within a system or across multiple systems. It tracks the origin of data, the transformations it undergoes, and how it is utilized across different processes or reports. Understanding data lineage is crucial for ensuring data integrity, tracing errors, and complying with regulatory requirements like GDPR or HIPAA. It also facilitates debugging of pipelines, audit trails for data governance, and helps analysts and data scientists understand how changes in source data can impact downstream analytics or models.

11. What is dimensionality reduction in data science?
Answer: Dimensionality reduction is a technique used to reduce the number of input variables in a dataset while preserving as much relevant information as possible. This helps in simplifying models, reducing computational cost, and avoiding the curse of dimensionality. Common methods include Principal Component Analysis (PCA), Linear Discriminant Analysis (LDA), and t-Distributed Stochastic Neighbor Embedding (t-SNE). These techniques help in visualizing high-dimensional data, improving model performance, and removing redundant or irrelevant features. It is an essential step in preprocessing large datasets in data science and machine learning workflows.

12. What is a confusion matrix and how is it useful?
Answer: A confusion matrix is a table used to evaluate the performance of a classification model by comparing actual and predicted labels. It consists of four outcomes: True Positive (TP), True Negative (TN), False Positive (FP), and False Negative (FN). This matrix helps in calculating various performance metrics such as accuracy, precision, recall, and F1-score. It provides a detailed breakdown of how well the model is performing across different classes. It is particularly useful when dealing with imbalanced datasets where accuracy alone can be misleading.

13. What is regularization in machine learning models?
Answer: Regularization is a technique used to prevent overfitting in machine learning models by adding a penalty term to the loss function. This discourages the model from fitting too closely to the training data, which can reduce its ability to generalize. Common types of regularization include L1 (Lasso) and L2 (Ridge) regularization. L1 tends to produce sparse models by eliminating less important features, while L2 penalizes large coefficients and maintains all features. Regularization improves model robustness and is widely used in linear regression, logistic regression, and neural networks.

14. How is k-means clustering different from hierarchical clustering?
Answer: K-means clustering is a partition-based algorithm that divides data into k predefined clusters by minimizing the variance within each cluster. It is fast and efficient but requires the number of clusters to be specified in advance. Hierarchical clustering, on the other hand, builds a tree-like structure of nested clusters without needing a predefined

number. It can be agglomerative (bottom-up) or divisive (top-down) and provides a dendrogram for visualization. While k-means is suitable for large datasets, hierarchical clustering offers better insights for smaller datasets and exploratory analysis.

15. What is the curse of dimensionality and why is it important?
Answer: The curse of dimensionality refers to the challenges and inefficiencies that arise when working with high-dimensional data. As the number of features increases, the data becomes sparse, distances between points become less meaningful, and the risk of overfitting increases. This affects the performance of machine learning algorithms, particularly those relying on distance metrics like k-NN. It also increases computational costs and complexity. To combat this, dimensionality reduction techniques and feature selection are applied. Understanding this concept is critical when designing models for large-scale data applications.

16. What is feature engineering in data science?
Answer: Feature engineering is the process of selecting, modifying, or creating new features from raw data to improve model performance. It includes techniques such as encoding categorical variables, normalization, discretization, and polynomial feature creation. Effective feature engineering can reveal hidden patterns, improve accuracy, and reduce the complexity of machine learning models. It is both an art and science that requires domain knowledge, creativity, and a solid understanding of statistical techniques. It plays a vital role in determining the success of data science projects.

17. What is the importance of cross-validation in model training?
Answer: Cross-validation is a statistical method used to evaluate the performance of machine learning models by splitting the dataset into multiple parts or folds. In k-fold cross-validation, the model is trained on $k-1$ folds and tested on the remaining fold. This process is repeated k times, and the results are averaged to reduce variability. Cross-validation helps detect overfitting, ensures model robustness, and provides a more accurate estimate of how the model will perform on unseen data. It is a fundamental technique for model validation and selection.

18. What is the difference between precision and recall?
Answer: Precision and recall are performance metrics used to evaluate classification models. Precision is the ratio of true positive predictions to the total predicted positives, reflecting the accuracy of positive predictions. Recall, or sensitivity, is the ratio of true positive predictions to all actual positives, measuring the model's ability to identify relevant instances. High precision means fewer false positives, while high recall means fewer false negatives. Depending on the application, one may be prioritized over the other. For example, recall is more important in medical diagnosis, whereas precision is crucial in spam detection.

19. How do decision trees work in classification problems?
Answer: Decision trees are a supervised learning algorithm used for classification and regression. They split the dataset into branches based on feature values, creating a tree-like structure where each node represents a decision point. The algorithm selects features that provide the highest information gain or Gini index at each step. The tree grows until it reaches a stopping criterion, such as maximum depth or minimum samples. Decision trees are easy to interpret, handle both numerical and categorical data, and can capture complex relationships. However, they are prone to overfitting and may require pruning or ensemble methods for improved performance.

20. What are ensemble learning methods in machine learning?
Answer: Ensemble learning involves combining multiple models to improve predictive performance, reduce variance, and increase robustness. Popular ensemble techniques include Bagging (e.g., Random Forest), Boosting (e.g., AdaBoost, XGBoost), and Stacking. Bagging reduces variance by training models on random subsets of data, while boosting improves accuracy by sequentially correcting errors made by previous models. Stacking involves training a meta-model on the outputs of base models. Ensemble methods often outperform individual models and are widely used in competitions and real-world applications for tasks like classification, regression, and anomaly detection.

21. What is the difference between parametric and non-parametric models?
Answer: Parametric models assume a fixed number of parameters and a specific functional form, such as linear regression or logistic regression. These models are easy to interpret and computationally efficient, but may not capture complex patterns if their assumptions are violated. Non-parametric models, like k-nearest neighbors or decision trees, make fewer assumptions about the data's distribution and can adapt to complex relationships. However, they may

require more data to perform well and are often more computationally intensive. Choosing between them depends on the dataset size, problem complexity, and interpretability requirements.

22. What is overfitting and how can it be prevented?
Answer: Overfitting occurs when a machine learning model learns not only the underlying patterns in the training data but also the noise, resulting in poor generalization to new data. It is often indicated by high training accuracy but low test accuracy. To prevent overfitting, techniques such as cross-validation, regularization (L1 or L2), pruning (for decision trees), dropout (in neural networks), and using simpler models can be employed. Collecting more data or reducing the number of features may also help. Addressing overfitting ensures a more robust and reliable model.

23. What are ROC curves and AUC in classification?
Answer: An ROC (Receiver Operating Characteristic) curve is a graphical representation of a classifier's performance across various thresholds, plotting the True Positive Rate (Recall) against the False Positive Rate. The AUC (Area Under the Curve) quantifies the overall ability of the model to distinguish between classes. A higher AUC indicates better model performance. ROC and AUC are particularly useful for evaluating models on imbalanced datasets, as they provide a more comprehensive view than accuracy alone. These tools help in selecting optimal thresholds and comparing different models.

24. What is a support vector machine (SVM)?
Answer: A Support Vector Machine (SVM) is a supervised learning algorithm used for classification and regression tasks. It works by finding the hyperplane that best separates data into classes while maximizing the margin between them. SVMs can handle linear and non-linear classification using kernel functions such as polynomial or radial basis function (RBF). They are effective in high-dimensional spaces and when the number of features exceeds the number of samples. SVMs are widely used in text classification, image recognition, and bioinformatics due to their robustness and accuracy.

25. What is the difference between batch and online learning?
Answer: Batch learning involves training a model on the entire dataset at once, making it suitable for static datasets where all data is available upfront. Online learning, also known as incremental learning, updates the model continuously as new data arrives, which is ideal for real-time systems or streaming data. Batch learning typically yields more stable models, while online learning is more memory-efficient and responsive. The choice depends on the data availability, application needs, and computational constraints.

26. What are principal components in PCA?
Answer: Principal components are new, uncorrelated variables formed by transforming the original variables in a dataset through Principal Component Analysis (PCA). They capture the maximum variance in the data and are ordered by importance, with the first few components retaining most of the data's information. PCA reduces dimensionality, removes multicollinearity, and simplifies visualization, especially for high-dimensional datasets. It is commonly used in exploratory data analysis, noise reduction, and as a preprocessing step in machine learning pipelines.

27. What is data normalization and why is it important?
Answer: Data normalization is the process of scaling numerical data into a standard range, typically between 0 and 1. It ensures that all features contribute equally to the model, preventing those with larger scales from dominating the outcome. Normalization is critical for distance-based algorithms like k-NN and clustering, as well as for gradient-based methods. Techniques include Min-Max Scaling and Z-score Standardization. Proper normalization improves model convergence, accuracy, and interpretability, especially when working with heterogeneous features.

28. What is the difference between classification and clustering?
Answer: Classification is a supervised learning task that assigns predefined labels to input data based on training with labeled examples. Clustering, on the other hand, is an unsupervised learning task that groups similar data points without prior labels. Classification predicts known categories (e.g., spam or not), while clustering discovers hidden patterns or segments (e.g., customer groups). Both are fundamental in data science, with classification used in diagnostics and fraud detection, and clustering used in market segmentation and anomaly detection.

29. What is feature selection and how is it different from feature extraction?
Answer: Feature selection involves choosing a subset of relevant features from the original dataset to improve model

performance and reduce complexity. It eliminates redundant or irrelevant variables using methods like filter, wrapper, or embedded techniques. Feature extraction, in contrast, creates new features by transforming or combining existing ones, as seen in PCA or autoencoders. While selection simplifies the model by retaining original features, extraction may generate more informative representations. Both are key in handling high-dimensional data and improving machine learning outcomes.

30. What is a random forest algorithm?
Answer: A Random Forest is an ensemble learning method that constructs multiple decision trees during training and outputs the mode of their predictions for classification or the average for regression. It reduces overfitting by averaging multiple trees trained on different subsets of the data and features. Random Forests are robust, easy to use, and handle missing values and categorical data well. They are commonly used in classification tasks like customer churn prediction, medical diagnosis, and credit scoring due to their high accuracy and interpretability.

31. What is a recommender system?
Answer: A recommender system is a machine learning application that suggests items to users based on their preferences or behavior. It is commonly used in e-commerce, streaming platforms, and social media. There are three main types: collaborative filtering (based on user-item interactions), content-based filtering (based on item features), and hybrid systems. Recommender systems improve user experience, increase engagement, and drive sales by providing personalized suggestions. They rely on data such as ratings, purchase history, and browsing patterns.

32. What is data leakage in machine learning?
Answer: Data leakage occurs when information from outside the training dataset is used to create the model, leading to overly optimistic performance and poor generalization. It can happen due to improper splitting of data, using future data, or including target-related features. Leakage undermines model validity and can lead to serious consequences in real-world applications. Preventing leakage involves careful preprocessing, maintaining temporal order, and ensuring that validation data is completely independent of training data.

33. What are hyperparameters and how are they tuned?
Answer: Hyperparameters are external configuration variables that define model structure or training process, such as learning rate, number of trees, or regularization strength. They are not learned from the data but must be set before training. Tuning hyperparameters optimizes model performance and generalization. Methods include Grid Search, Random Search, and Bayesian Optimization. Proper tuning can significantly improve accuracy and reduce overfitting, making it a critical part of model development and deployment.

34. What is a generative model in data science?
Answer: A generative model learns the underlying distribution of data and can generate new, similar data points. Unlike discriminative models that only classify input, generative models aim to understand how the data was generated. Examples include Gaussian Mixture Models, Variational Autoencoders, and Generative Adversarial Networks (GANs). These models are used in tasks like image synthesis, text generation, and anomaly detection. They provide deeper insights into the data structure and are essential in unsupervised learning and data augmentation.

35. What is the role of Big Data in Data Science?
Answer: Big Data provides the large, diverse datasets necessary for training robust data science models. It enables the discovery of hidden patterns, trends, and correlations that small datasets cannot reveal. Big Data technologies like Hadoop, Spark, and NoSQL databases facilitate the storage, processing, and analysis of massive datasets across distributed systems. In data science, Big Data supports real-time analytics, predictive modeling, and data-driven decision-making in areas like healthcare, finance, and IoT. It is the backbone of modern analytics and machine learning applications.

36. What is MapReduce in big data processing?
Answer: MapReduce is a programming model used for processing and generating large datasets across distributed clusters. It consists of two main functions: Map, which processes and filters data, and Reduce, which aggregates the results. Developed by Google, MapReduce enables parallel processing and fault-tolerant data handling in systems like Hadoop. It is ideal for batch processing of log data, web indexing, and large-scale data transformation. Although newer technologies like Spark offer faster alternatives, MapReduce remains foundational in big data frameworks.

37. What is a NoSQL database and when is it used?

Answer: NoSQL databases are non-relational databases designed for handling large volumes of unstructured or semi-structured data. Unlike traditional SQL databases, they offer flexible schemas and horizontal scalability. Types include document (MongoDB), key-value (Redis), columnar (Cassandra), and graph databases (Neo4j). NoSQL is used in scenarios requiring high-speed data access, real-time analytics, and scalability, such as social media, IoT, and recommendation engines. It enables developers to store and retrieve complex data types without predefined schemas.

38. What is the difference between Hadoop and Spark?

Answer: Hadoop and Spark are both big data processing frameworks, but they differ in architecture and performance. Hadoop uses MapReduce for batch processing and stores data in HDFS (Hadoop Distributed File System). Spark offers in-memory processing, which makes it significantly faster for iterative tasks and real-time analytics. Spark also provides libraries for machine learning (MLlib), streaming (Spark Streaming), and graph processing (GraphX), making it more versatile. While Hadoop is suited for long-running batch jobs, Spark is preferred for interactive, real-time applications.

39. What are the characteristics of Big Data?

Answer: Big Data is typically described by the five V's: Volume (large data size), Velocity (speed of generation), Variety (different types and sources), Veracity (data quality and accuracy), and Value (usefulness of the data). These characteristics define the complexity and challenges of managing Big Data. Understanding these aspects helps in selecting appropriate tools and designing efficient data processing architectures. The five V's also highlight the importance of Big Data in deriving insights and driving innovation.

40. What is stream processing in Big Data?

Answer: Stream processing refers to the real-time processing of data as it is generated. Unlike batch processing, which deals with static data sets, stream processing handles continuous data flows from sources like sensors, logs, or financial transactions. Technologies like Apache Kafka, Apache Flink, and Apache Storm enable stream processing for tasks like fraud detection, real-time analytics, and monitoring. It is crucial in time-sensitive applications where immediate insights are required. Stream processing enhances responsiveness and supports low-latency decision-making in Big Data systems.

41. How does Natural Language Processing (NLP) contribute to Big Data analytics?

Answer: Natural Language Processing (NLP) plays a crucial role in Big Data analytics by enabling machines to understand, interpret, and generate human language. It helps in extracting meaningful insights from unstructured text data such as social media posts, emails, customer reviews, and more. NLP techniques like sentiment analysis, named entity recognition, and topic modeling help businesses gauge customer sentiments, automate support, and identify trends. It supports multilingual data handling and improves human-computer interaction. In Big Data contexts, NLP enhances the value extracted from large volumes of text, making data-driven decisions more informed and contextual.

42. What is the purpose of a confusion matrix in classification problems?

Answer: A confusion matrix is a performance evaluation tool used in classification problems to summarize the results of a model's predictions. It presents a tabular layout of actual versus predicted classifications, divided into True Positives, False Positives, True Negatives, and False Negatives. This matrix helps in calculating important metrics such as accuracy, precision, recall, and F1-score. It provides a deeper understanding of the model's behavior, especially in imbalanced datasets, by highlighting where the model performs well and where it fails. It is essential for evaluating and improving classification models in data science.

43. What is Feature Engineering, and why is it important?

Answer: Feature engineering is the process of transforming raw data into meaningful features that enhance the performance of machine learning models. It involves selecting, modifying, or creating new features from existing data to improve model accuracy. Techniques include normalization, encoding categorical variables, and creating interaction terms. Feature engineering is crucial because the quality of input features often determines the effectiveness of a model. Well-crafted features simplify complex patterns, reduce overfitting, and increase predictive power. It bridges the gap between raw data and machine learning algorithms, making it a vital skill in data science.

44. What is data wrangling in Data Science?
Answer: Data wrangling, also known as data munging, is the process of cleaning, transforming, and organizing raw data into a structured format suitable for analysis. It involves handling missing values, correcting data types, removing duplicates, and normalizing inconsistent formats. The goal is to prepare data so that it can be easily analyzed or fed into machine learning models. Data wrangling is a foundational step in any data science workflow, as real-world data is often messy and unstructured. Efficient data wrangling ensures the accuracy and quality of insights derived from analytics.

45. What are ROC and AUC in the context of model evaluation?
Answer: ROC (Receiver Operating Characteristic) curve is a graphical representation of a classifier's performance across different thresholds, plotting the True Positive Rate against the False Positive Rate. AUC (Area Under the Curve) quantifies the overall ability of the model to discriminate between classes. An AUC value closer to 1 indicates excellent performance, while 0.5 suggests no discriminative power. ROC-AUC is particularly useful for imbalanced datasets and when comparing multiple models. It provides a comprehensive measure of model quality, beyond just accuracy, helping data scientists select the most effective model.

46. What is the significance of data pipelines in Big Data processing?
Answer: Data pipelines are automated workflows that transport, transform, and store data from multiple sources to a destination system for analysis or storage. In Big Data, they handle large-scale, continuous data flows efficiently. Pipelines consist of stages like data ingestion, cleansing, transformation, and loading (ETL). They ensure timely and consistent data delivery, minimize manual errors, and support real-time processing. Technologies like Apache NiFi, Kafka, and Airflow are commonly used for building pipelines. Data pipelines are essential for scalable and reliable data infrastructure in Big Data environments, enabling seamless analytics and decision-making.

47. What is Apache Hive, and how is it used in Big Data?
Answer: Apache Hive is a data warehouse software built on top of Hadoop that allows users to query and manage large datasets stored in HDFS using a SQL-like language called HiveQL. It abstracts the complexity of writing MapReduce jobs and simplifies data analysis for users familiar with SQL. Hive is optimized for batch processing and is used for reporting, data summarization, and analysis on massive datasets. It supports integration with tools like Apache Tez and Spark for enhanced performance. Hive democratizes access to Big Data, enabling structured querying over unstructured data efficiently.

48. What are the challenges in implementing IoT with Big Data?
Answer: Integrating IoT with Big Data presents several challenges, including data volume, variety, and velocity due to the massive number of connected devices generating continuous streams. Ensuring data security and privacy is a significant concern, especially with sensitive sensor data. Other challenges include real-time data processing, managing heterogeneous data formats, network reliability, and the scalability of storage and analytics infrastructure. Additionally, integrating legacy systems and ensuring standardization across devices are complex tasks. Addressing these challenges requires robust architecture, edge computing, advanced analytics tools, and strong data governance policies.

49. What is edge computing, and how does it relate to IoT?
Answer: Edge computing refers to the practice of processing data near the source of generation, such as IoT sensors or devices, rather than sending it to centralized servers or cloud platforms. It reduces latency, minimizes bandwidth usage, and enhances response time for time-sensitive applications. In the context of IoT, edge computing enables real-time analytics, device control, and data filtering before transmission. This is crucial for applications like autonomous vehicles, industrial automation, and remote monitoring. By decentralizing computation, edge computing enhances performance, reliability, and security in IoT ecosystems.

50. What is the purpose of data governance in Big Data and IoT systems?
Answer: Data governance encompasses the policies, standards, and procedures that ensure the effective and secure management of data throughout its lifecycle. In Big Data and IoT systems, where vast and varied data is generated continuously, governance ensures data quality, privacy, compliance, and accountability. It defines roles, responsibilities, and data access controls. Proper data governance prevents unauthorized use, supports regulatory compliance (like GDPR), and maintains data integrity across systems. As IoT devices generate critical real-time data, governance frameworks are essential for reliable decision-making and secure, ethical use of information.

51. What is the role of natural language processing (NLP) in data science?
Answer: NLP, or Natural Language Processing, plays a critical role in data science by enabling computers to understand, interpret, and generate human language. It allows data scientists to process large volumes of unstructured text data from sources like social media, customer reviews, and news articles. Key NLP tasks include sentiment analysis, text classification, named entity recognition, and machine translation. By using NLP, organizations can gain valuable insights from textual data, automate communication systems, and improve decision-making. NLP also integrates with AI and machine learning models to power chatbots, virtual assistants, and recommendation systems, making it a vital tool in modern data-driven applications.

52. What is dimensionality reduction in big data?
Answer: Dimensionality reduction is the process of reducing the number of input variables in a dataset while retaining essential information. In big data, datasets often contain hundreds or thousands of features, which can lead to overfitting, slow computation, and complex visualization. Techniques like Principal Component Analysis (PCA), t-SNE, and autoencoders are commonly used for dimensionality reduction. This process helps in improving model performance, reducing noise, and enhancing visualization. It also aids in identifying the most significant variables that influence the output. Dimensionality reduction is especially useful in image processing, genomics, and natural language processing.

53. What is the difference between regression and classification?
Answer: Regression and classification are two types of supervised learning techniques in machine learning. Regression is used when the output variable is continuous and involves predicting numerical values, such as predicting house prices or temperature. Classification, on the other hand, deals with categorical outputs and involves assigning data points to predefined classes, like spam vs. non-spam emails or disease diagnosis. The evaluation metrics also differ—regression uses RMSE or MAE, while classification uses accuracy, precision, and recall. Both are essential in data science but are applied depending on the nature of the target variable.

54. How does cross-validation help in model evaluation?
Answer: Cross-validation is a technique used to assess the performance of a machine learning model by splitting the dataset into multiple training and validation sets. The most common form is k-fold cross-validation, where the data is divided into k subsets, and the model is trained and validated k times, each time using a different subset as the validation set. This approach helps in reducing overfitting, ensures that the model generalizes well to unseen data, and provides a more robust estimate of performance. It is especially useful when working with limited datasets, offering a more reliable alternative to simple train-test splits.

55. What are the key challenges in processing big data?
Answer: Processing big data poses several challenges including volume, velocity, and variety—the three V's of big data. Volume refers to the massive size of datasets, requiring scalable storage and processing. Velocity deals with the speed of data generation and the need for real-time processing. Variety refers to the different formats like structured, semi-structured, and unstructured data. Other challenges include ensuring data quality, maintaining data privacy and security, integrating heterogeneous data sources, and selecting the right tools and infrastructure. Efficient handling of big data requires robust architecture, advanced algorithms, and parallel processing frameworks like Hadoop and Spark.

56. What is the difference between Hadoop and Spark?
Answer: Hadoop and Spark are both big data processing frameworks, but they differ significantly. Hadoop uses MapReduce, which writes intermediate results to disk, making it slower. Spark, on the other hand, processes data in memory, which leads to faster computation. Spark supports batch processing, real-time streaming, machine learning, and graph processing, while Hadoop primarily handles batch jobs. In terms of ease of use, Spark offers high-level APIs in Python, Scala, and Java, and includes libraries like MLlib for machine learning. Hadoop is more storage-focused with HDFS, whereas Spark emphasizes in-memory computation and faster data analytics.

57. What is a NoSQL database, and why is it used in big data?
Answer: A NoSQL database is a non-relational database designed to handle large volumes of unstructured or semi-structured data. Unlike traditional SQL databases, NoSQL databases do not use fixed table schemas and are highly scalable, making them ideal for big data applications. Common types include document stores (e.g., MongoDB), key-value stores (e.g., Redis), column stores (e.g., Cassandra), and graph databases (e.g., Neo4j). NoSQL databases

provide flexibility in data modeling, support horizontal scaling, and offer high performance for distributed computing environments. They are widely used in real-time web applications, IoT platforms, and social networks.

58. What are data lakes and how do they differ from data warehouses?

Answer: A data lake is a centralized repository that stores raw, unprocessed data in its native format, while a data warehouse stores structured, cleaned, and processed data. Data lakes are built on technologies like Hadoop and cloud storage, supporting various data types such as logs, images, videos, and documents. They are more flexible and scalable but require strong governance. Data warehouses, on the other hand, use predefined schemas and are optimized for fast SQL queries and business intelligence tools. Data lakes are preferred for exploratory data science, whereas data warehouses are ideal for reporting and analytics.

59. What is MapReduce and how does it work?

Answer: MapReduce is a programming model used for processing large datasets in a distributed environment. It consists of two main functions: the Map function, which processes input data and converts it into key-value pairs, and the Reduce function, which aggregates or summarizes the output from the Map phase. MapReduce is designed to run on clusters of computers, allowing for parallel data processing. It is fault-tolerant, scalable, and forms the core processing engine in the Hadoop ecosystem. Despite its simplicity, MapReduce can handle complex analytical tasks over massive datasets, making it essential in big data processing.

60. What is the role of edge computing in IoT?

Answer: Edge computing in IoT involves processing data near the source of generation, such as sensors or smart devices, instead of sending it to centralized data centers or clouds. This approach reduces latency, conserves bandwidth, and improves real-time responsiveness. In critical applications like autonomous vehicles, healthcare monitoring, and industrial automation, edge computing ensures quicker decision-making and enhanced data privacy. It also alleviates the load on cloud infrastructure. By distributing computation closer to the "edge" of the network, edge computing enhances efficiency and reliability in large-scale IoT deployments.

61. What is feature engineering and why is it important in data science?

Answer: Feature engineering is the process of selecting, modifying, and creating variables (features) from raw data to improve the performance of machine learning models. It involves techniques like normalization, encoding categorical variables, creating interaction terms, and handling missing data. Good feature engineering transforms data into formats that make patterns more detectable by algorithms. It plays a critical role in model accuracy, interpretability, and training efficiency. Without effective feature engineering, even the most advanced models may perform poorly. It requires domain knowledge, creativity, and a deep understanding of the data.

62. What is overfitting in machine learning and how can it be prevented?

Answer: Overfitting occurs when a machine learning model learns the noise or random fluctuations in the training data instead of the underlying pattern. This results in excellent performance on training data but poor generalization to new, unseen data. It can be prevented using techniques such as cross-validation, regularization (like L1 or L2), pruning decision trees, simplifying the model, or using more training data. Additionally, early stopping during training and using ensemble methods like bagging or boosting can help mitigate overfitting. Preventing overfitting is essential for building robust and reliable predictive models.

63. What is streaming data and how is it handled in big data analytics?

Answer: Streaming data refers to continuous flows of data generated in real time by sources such as IoT sensors, social media, financial transactions, or web logs. Handling streaming data requires specialized tools and frameworks capable of real-time ingestion, processing, and analysis. Technologies like Apache Kafka, Apache Flink, Apache Storm, and Spark Streaming are commonly used. These tools provide mechanisms for low-latency processing, fault tolerance, and scalability. Streaming analytics enables real-time decision-making, fraud detection, predictive maintenance, and more. It is a key aspect of modern big data infrastructure.

64. How does data anonymization work in data science?

Answer: Data anonymization is the process of modifying personal data so that individuals cannot be identified, directly or indirectly. Techniques include masking, generalization, randomization, and pseudonymization. It is crucial for complying with data protection laws like GDPR and HIPAA. Anonymization ensures that data remains useful for analysis while protecting user privacy. However, care must be taken to prevent re-identification, especially when combining multiple datasets. Effective anonymization balances data utility with privacy and is essential in healthcare, finance, and social science research involving sensitive data.

65. What are recommendation systems and how do they work?
Answer: Recommendation systems are algorithms designed to suggest relevant items to users based on preferences, behaviors, or similarities. They are widely used in e-commerce, streaming services, and social media. There are three main types: content-based filtering (recommends items similar to those the user liked), collaborative filtering (recommends based on preferences of similar users), and hybrid models that combine both. These systems use data like user ratings, purchase history, and browsing behavior. Effective recommendation systems enhance user engagement, increase sales, and improve customer satisfaction.

66. What is a confusion matrix in machine learning and how is it used?
Answer: A confusion matrix is a performance evaluation tool used for classification models. It is a 2x2 (or more for multiclass problems) table that shows the actual versus predicted classifications. The main components are True Positives (TP), True Negatives (TN), False Positives (FP), and False Negatives (FN). From these, various metrics such as accuracy, precision, recall, and F1-score can be derived. For example, precision = TP / (TP + FP), and recall = TP / (TP + FN). The confusion matrix provides a deeper insight into the types of errors a model is making and is essential for tuning classification models, especially when dealing with imbalanced datasets.

67. What is ROC-AUC, and why is it important in model evaluation?
Answer: ROC-AUC (Receiver Operating Characteristic - Area Under the Curve) is a metric used to evaluate the performance of a binary classification model. The ROC curve plots the True Positive Rate against the False Positive Rate at various threshold settings. The AUC value quantifies the overall ability of the model to discriminate between the positive and negative classes. An AUC of 1.0 indicates perfect classification, while 0.5 suggests random guessing. It is particularly useful when working with imbalanced datasets, as it evaluates the classifier's performance across all classification thresholds, giving a comprehensive view beyond just accuracy.

68. What is hyperparameter tuning in machine learning?
Answer: Hyperparameter tuning involves selecting the optimal set of parameters that govern the learning process of a machine learning algorithm. Unlike model parameters learned during training (like weights in a neural network), hyperparameters are set before training, such as learning rate, number of trees, or regularization strength. Techniques like Grid Search, Random Search, and Bayesian Optimization are commonly used for tuning. Proper hyperparameter tuning can significantly improve model accuracy and performance by finding the best combination of settings that reduce underfitting or overfitting.

69. What are some common feature engineering techniques?
Answer: Feature engineering is the process of transforming raw data into meaningful input features to improve model performance. Common techniques include normalization and scaling (e.g., Min-Max or Z-score), encoding categorical variables (one-hot, label encoding), creating interaction terms, binning continuous variables, handling missing values, extracting date-time features, and dimensionality reduction (PCA, LDA). These transformations help models learn better by highlighting important patterns, improving convergence, and enabling algorithms to handle diverse data types effectively.

70. What is cross-validation, and why is it used?
Answer: Cross-validation is a technique for assessing the generalizability of a machine learning model by dividing the data into multiple training and validation sets. The most common form is k-fold cross-validation, where the data is split into 'k' parts, with each part used once as the validation set while the others form the training set. This helps mitigate overfitting, provides a better estimate of model performance, and ensures that the model performs well on unseen data. It is especially useful when working with limited data and when tuning hyperparameters.

71. What is the purpose of normalization and standardization in data preprocessing?
Answer: Normalization and standardization are techniques used to scale numerical data features so they contribute equally to the model's learning process. Normalization (Min-Max scaling) rescales features to a fixed range, usually [0, 1]. Standardization (Z-score scaling) transforms features to have zero mean and unit variance. These techniques are crucial for models sensitive to the magnitude of input features, such as gradient descent-based algorithms or

distance-based models like k-NN and SVM. Scaling improves convergence speed, prevents dominance by high-magnitude features, and leads to more reliable models.

72. What is the curse of dimensionality?
Answer: The curse of dimensionality refers to various issues that arise when analyzing and organizing data in high-dimensional spaces. As the number of features (dimensions) increases, the data becomes sparse, and the volume of the space increases exponentially. This makes distance metrics less meaningful, increases computation time, and can lead to overfitting. In high dimensions, models struggle to generalize well because training data is insufficient to cover the vast feature space. Techniques such as dimensionality reduction (PCA) or feature selection are used to mitigate this issue.

73. What is the importance of data visualization in data science?
Answer: Data visualization plays a crucial role in data science by enabling the effective communication of data insights, patterns, and trends. Through charts, graphs, heatmaps, and dashboards, it simplifies complex datasets, highlights outliers, and supports exploratory data analysis. Visualization tools like Matplotlib, Seaborn, Tableau, and Power BI help in decision-making and storytelling. It is also essential for validating assumptions, understanding feature relationships, and presenting results to stakeholders who may not be technically inclined. Good visualizations often lead to faster insights and better model understanding.

74. What is an outlier and how is it treated in data preprocessing?
Answer: An outlier is a data point that significantly deviates from other observations in the dataset. It can result from data entry errors, measurement variability, or rare events. Outliers can skew statistical analyses, mislead models, and reduce prediction accuracy. Detection methods include box plots, Z-score, IQR, or clustering techniques. Depending on the context, outliers can be removed, transformed (e.g., log transformation), or imputed. Proper handling of outliers is crucial in maintaining model performance and ensuring that patterns are not biased or misrepresented.

75. What is principal component analysis (PCA)?
Answer: Principal Component Analysis (PCA) is an unsupervised linear dimensionality reduction technique used to reduce the number of input features while retaining most of the original variance in the data. PCA works by identifying directions (principal components) that capture the maximum variance and projecting data onto them. It helps in visualizing high-dimensional data, improving model performance by removing multicollinearity, and speeding up computation. PCA is widely used in preprocessing steps for clustering, classification, and anomaly detection tasks, especially when dealing with large, correlated datasets.

76. What is the difference between classification and clustering?
Answer: Classification and clustering are both tasks in machine learning, but they differ in purpose and methodology. Classification is a supervised learning task where the model learns from labeled data to assign new instances into predefined categories (e.g., spam vs. not spam). Clustering, on the other hand, is an unsupervised learning task that involves grouping similar instances together based on patterns in the data without predefined labels (e.g., customer segmentation). While classification predicts known outputs, clustering uncovers hidden structures and insights from raw data.

77. What is time series forecasting?
Answer: Time series forecasting involves predicting future values based on historical data collected over time. It is commonly used in financial markets, weather prediction, sales forecasting, and more. Time series data has sequential order and may exhibit trends, seasonality, and autocorrelation. Models like ARIMA, SARIMA, Prophet, and LSTM neural networks are widely used for forecasting. Accurate time series forecasting enables better planning, resource allocation, and risk management by providing insights into expected future behaviors or events.

78. What is ensemble learning in machine learning?
Answer: Ensemble learning is a technique that combines multiple models (often called "weak learners") to create a more accurate and robust prediction model. The key idea is that a group of weak learners, when combined, can outperform a single strong learner. Popular ensemble methods include Bagging (e.g., Random Forest), Boosting (e.g., AdaBoost, XGBoost), and Stacking. Ensemble models reduce variance, bias, or both, leading to improved model performance and generalization, especially in complex or noisy datasets.

79. What is the role of an API in IoT systems?
Answer: An API (Application Programming Interface) serves as a communication bridge between different software applications in an IoT ecosystem. It allows devices, servers, and apps to send and receive data, triggering actions or updating states. APIs are essential for integrating sensors, gateways, cloud services, and user interfaces. They ensure interoperability across platforms and enable developers to build scalable and flexible systems. RESTful APIs and MQTT protocols are commonly used in IoT for lightweight, real-time data exchange. Proper API management enhances security, reliability, and performance in IoT solutions.

80. What is MQTT, and why is it used in IoT?
Answer: MQTT (Message Queuing Telemetry Transport) is a lightweight, publish-subscribe messaging protocol designed for low-bandwidth, high-latency, or unreliable networks—making it ideal for IoT applications. It enables communication between devices and servers with minimal resource consumption. In MQTT, devices publish messages to a broker under specific topics, and other devices subscribe to receive those messages. MQTT is efficient, secure, and widely supported in IoT platforms. Its ability to ensure real-time, scalable, and bi-directional communication makes it a preferred protocol for remote sensing, home automation, and industrial IoT deployments.

81. What is a recommender system and how does it work?
Answer: A recommender system is an algorithmic tool used to suggest items (like movies, products, or books) to users based on their preferences and behavior. It works using techniques such as content-based filtering (recommending items similar to what the user liked before), collaborative filtering (recommending based on similar users' preferences), or hybrid approaches that combine both. Recommender systems utilize user-item interaction data, ratings, and behavioral patterns to personalize experiences and increase user engagement, commonly seen in platforms like Netflix, Amazon, and Spotify.

82. What is Natural Language Processing (NLP) in data science?
Answer: Natural Language Processing (NLP) is a subfield of AI and data science that focuses on the interaction between computers and human languages. It enables machines to understand, interpret, and generate human language. Applications include sentiment analysis, language translation, chatbots, text summarization, and speech recognition. NLP combines computational linguistics, machine learning, and deep learning to process unstructured text data. Libraries like NLTK, spaCy, and Transformers are commonly used tools in NLP projects, facilitating automated understanding of large volumes of text.

83. What is the difference between structured and unstructured data?
Answer: Structured data is highly organized and easily searchable in relational databases with defined formats (like tables), consisting of rows and columns—for example, customer records or transaction logs. Unstructured data lacks a predefined format, making it harder to process and analyze—examples include emails, videos, social media posts, and sensor data. Data science tools and techniques differ for both types: structured data is handled using SQL, while unstructured data often requires machine learning, NLP, or big data tools for effective analysis.

84. What is Hadoop and how does it work in big data processing?
Answer: Hadoop is an open-source framework designed to store and process large-scale datasets across distributed computing environments. It works through two main components: the Hadoop Distributed File System (HDFS), which stores data across multiple machines, and the MapReduce programming model, which processes data in parallel. Hadoop enables fault tolerance, scalability, and cost-effectiveness, making it suitable for analyzing massive volumes of structured or unstructured data. It is widely used in big data analytics pipelines and serves as the foundation for modern big data ecosystems.

85. What is the use of Spark in data science?
Answer: Apache Spark is an open-source data processing framework designed for speed and scalability in handling big data workloads. Unlike traditional MapReduce, Spark performs in-memory computation, making it faster for iterative machine learning tasks. It supports APIs in Python, Scala, Java, and R and includes modules for SQL processing, streaming, machine learning (MLlib), and graph processing (GraphX). Spark is widely used for real-time analytics, ETL jobs, and machine learning workflows in big data environments due to its flexibility and performance.

86. What is a NoSQL database, and how is it different from SQL?
Answer: A NoSQL database is a non-relational database designed to handle a wide variety of data formats, especially

large volumes of unstructured or semi-structured data. Unlike SQL databases, which use tables and schemas, NoSQL databases support key-value, document, column-family, or graph data models. Examples include MongoDB, Cassandra, and Redis. NoSQL databases offer high scalability, flexibility, and performance for big data applications, making them suitable for real-time web apps, IoT systems, and content management where data structure is dynamic or unknown.

87. What is batch processing in big data?
Answer: Batch processing refers to executing a series of jobs on large datasets without manual intervention. It processes data in blocks or batches at scheduled intervals. This approach is suitable for applications where real-time response is not required, such as payroll, billing systems, or nightly data warehousing updates. Technologies like Apache Hadoop and Spark support batch processing through MapReduce and Spark jobs. Batch processing is reliable and efficient for handling repetitive, high-volume data operations over a set time frame.

88. What is real-time processing, and where is it used?
Answer: Real-time processing involves analyzing and responding to data immediately as it is generated. It is critical in use cases like fraud detection, online recommendation systems, stock trading platforms, and IoT systems. Tools such as Apache Kafka, Apache Storm, and Spark Streaming enable real-time data ingestion and processing. Real-time systems are built for low-latency and high-throughput performance, ensuring timely insights and actions based on streaming data, as opposed to batch processing which analyzes data in chunks after collection.

89. What is data wrangling in data science?
Answer: Data wrangling, also known as data munging, is the process of cleaning, transforming, and preparing raw data into a structured and usable format for analysis. It involves tasks such as handling missing values, removing duplicates, converting data types, and normalizing values. Data wrangling is a crucial step in any data science pipeline, as real-world data is often messy and inconsistent. Tools like Pandas, OpenRefine, and Excel help data scientists efficiently preprocess data for machine learning and statistical modeling.

90. What are the challenges of working with big data?
Answer: Working with big data presents several challenges including data volume (storage and processing), velocity (real-time streaming), variety (structured and unstructured formats), and veracity (data accuracy and consistency). Additional challenges involve ensuring data privacy, scalability of infrastructure, managing distributed systems, and integration with legacy systems. Solutions require robust data pipelines, cloud computing resources, distributed processing frameworks (like Hadoop and Spark), and strong data governance practices to extract reliable and actionable insights from vast and complex datasets.

91. What is text mining, and how is it applied in data science?
Answer: Text mining is the process of deriving meaningful information from unstructured textual data using statistical, linguistic, and machine learning techniques. It includes tasks like keyword extraction, sentiment analysis, document classification, and topic modeling. Text mining is widely used in applications such as opinion mining from social media, customer feedback analysis, and document summarization. NLP libraries like NLTK and spaCy are commonly used in text mining projects, enabling businesses and researchers to unlock insights from large volumes of text data.

92. What is a knowledge graph in data science?
Answer: A knowledge graph is a data structure that represents relationships among entities using nodes (entities) and edges (relationships). It provides a semantic, connected view of data, enabling machines to understand context and meaning. Knowledge graphs are used in search engines, recommendation systems, and natural language understanding. Google's Knowledge Graph is a well-known example, enhancing search results with structured facts. In data science, knowledge graphs help integrate diverse datasets, perform reasoning, and uncover insights through graph analytics.

93. What is the concept of edge computing in IoT and big data?
Answer: Edge computing refers to processing data closer to the source (like IoT devices or edge servers) rather than relying on centralized cloud systems. It reduces latency, conserves bandwidth, and enables real-time decision-making. In big data and IoT, edge computing is essential for applications such as autonomous vehicles, industrial automation, and smart cities. By offloading computation to the edge, systems can react faster and operate efficiently even with intermittent connectivity to central servers or cloud services.

94. What is blockchain's role in data science and IoT?
Answer: Blockchain provides a decentralized, tamper-proof ledger system that enhances data integrity, transparency, and security. In IoT, blockchain ensures secure communication between devices, tracks transactions, and prevents unauthorized access. In data science, blockchain can verify data provenance, ensuring that analytical insights are based on trustworthy data. Combining blockchain with big data analytics allows organizations to build secure, traceable, and auditable systems, particularly useful in industries like finance, healthcare, and supply chain.

95. What is anomaly detection, and where is it applied?
Answer: Anomaly detection involves identifying rare or unexpected patterns in data that do not conform to expected behavior. It is applied in fraud detection, network security, equipment monitoring, and healthcare diagnostics. Techniques include statistical methods, clustering, and machine learning algorithms like Isolation Forest, One-Class SVM, or Autoencoders. Effective anomaly detection helps in early issue identification, risk mitigation, and system reliability by flagging outliers that may indicate errors, threats, or unusual activities.

96. What is transfer learning in deep learning?
Answer: Transfer learning is a deep learning technique where a model developed for one task is reused as the starting point for another related task. It is particularly useful when labeled data is scarce. For example, a model trained on a large image dataset like ImageNet can be fine-tuned to classify specific types of medical images. Transfer learning significantly reduces training time, computational resources, and improves performance in cases where direct training from scratch would be inefficient or impractical.

97. What is data lake in big data architecture?
Answer: A data lake is a centralized repository that allows storing structured, semi-structured, and unstructured data at scale in its raw format. Unlike data warehouses, which require structured data with predefined schema, data lakes offer flexibility for data scientists to explore and analyze diverse data types using big data tools like Hadoop or Spark. Data lakes support advanced analytics, machine learning, and real-time processing, making them ideal for storing IoT data, logs, multimedia, and documents.

98. What is the use of feature selection in model building?
Answer: Feature selection involves choosing the most relevant input features for building a predictive model. It improves model performance by reducing overfitting, training time, and complexity. Techniques include filter methods (e.g., correlation), wrapper methods (e.g., recursive feature elimination), and embedded methods (e.g., Lasso). Selecting the right features ensures that the model focuses on variables with the most predictive power, leading to better accuracy and interpretability while discarding irrelevant or redundant data.

99. What is the use of confusion matrix in model evaluation?
Answer: A confusion matrix is a performance measurement tool for classification models. It provides insights into the number of true positives, false positives, true negatives, and false negatives. From this matrix, metrics like accuracy, precision, recall, and F1-score can be derived. The confusion matrix helps identify types of classification errors and is especially useful for imbalanced datasets where accuracy alone can be misleading. It provides a more detailed analysis of how well the model distinguishes between classes.

100. What is correlation and how is it used in data analysis?
Answer: Correlation measures the statistical relationship between two variables, indicating how changes in one variable relate to changes in another. It ranges from -1 to +1, where +1 implies a perfect positive relationship, -1 a perfect negative relationship, and 0 no relationship. Correlation analysis helps identify multicollinearity among features, assists in feature selection, and provides insights into variable dependencies. It is commonly visualized using heatmaps or scatter plots during exploratory data analysis in data science projects.

101. What is dimensionality reduction in data science?
Answer: Dimensionality reduction is the process of reducing the number of input variables or features in a dataset while preserving as much relevant information as possible. This helps in improving model performance, reducing overfitting, and enhancing visualization. Techniques such as Principal Component Analysis (PCA), t-SNE, and Linear Discriminant Analysis (LDA) are commonly used. By eliminating redundant or irrelevant features, dimensionality reduction makes data easier to interpret and computationally more efficient, especially in high-dimensional datasets.

102. What is a heatmap and where is it used in data science?
Answer: A heatmap is a data visualization tool that represents data values through color gradients. It is commonly used to show the correlation between features in a dataset, highlighting positive, negative, or neutral relationships. Heatmaps are valuable during exploratory data analysis (EDA), especially when working with large datasets, as they quickly identify strong correlations, outliers, and trends. Libraries such as Seaborn and Matplotlib in Python are widely used for creating heatmaps.

103. What are activation functions in neural networks?
Answer: Activation functions introduce non-linearity into the neural network, allowing it to learn complex patterns. They determine the output of each neuron given an input. Common activation functions include Sigmoid, Tanh, ReLU (Rectified Linear Unit), and Softmax. ReLU is widely used in hidden layers due to its simplicity and efficiency, while Softmax is used in the output layer for classification problems. Choosing the right activation function is crucial for effective learning and convergence of the network.

104. What is backpropagation in deep learning?
Answer: Backpropagation is the algorithm used to train neural networks by minimizing the loss function. It works by propagating the error backward from the output layer to the input layer, adjusting the weights using gradient descent. This process helps the model learn from its mistakes by updating parameters to reduce the difference between predicted and actual values. Backpropagation is essential for efficient and accurate learning in deep learning architectures.

105. What is hyperparameter tuning in machine learning?
Answer: Hyperparameter tuning involves selecting the optimal values for model parameters that are not learned from data but are set before the training process. Examples include learning rate, number of trees in a random forest, or number of hidden layers in a neural network. Techniques like Grid Search, Random Search, and Bayesian Optimization are used to find the best combination of hyperparameters, improving model performance and avoiding underfitting or overfitting.

106. What is ensemble learning and its types?
Answer: Ensemble learning is a technique that combines multiple models to produce better predictive performance than a single model. The main types of ensemble learning are Bagging (e.g., Random Forest), Boosting (e.g., XGBoost, AdaBoost), and Stacking. Bagging reduces variance, boosting reduces bias, and stacking combines different types of models to leverage their strengths. Ensemble methods are widely used in competitive machine learning and real-world applications due to their high accuracy and robustness.

107. What is cross-validation and why is it important?
Answer: Cross-validation is a technique for assessing the generalizability of a model by dividing the dataset into multiple training and testing subsets. The most common method is k-fold cross-validation, where the data is split into k parts and the model is trained and tested k times. It helps prevent overfitting and ensures that the model performs well on unseen data, providing a more reliable estimate of model accuracy and performance.

108. What is overfitting and how can it be avoided?
Answer: Overfitting occurs when a model learns the training data too well, including noise and outliers, resulting in poor generalization to new data. It can be avoided using techniques like cross-validation, regularization (L1/L2), pruning (in decision trees), dropout (in neural networks), and by using simpler models. Monitoring validation loss and using early stopping during training also help prevent overfitting. Balancing model complexity and data representation is key to avoiding this issue.

109. What is the difference between bagging and boosting?
Answer: Bagging (Bootstrap Aggregating) and Boosting are both ensemble learning methods, but they differ in approach. Bagging builds multiple independent models in parallel on random subsets of the training data and averages their outputs to reduce variance. Boosting builds models sequentially, where each new model focuses on correcting the errors made by the previous ones, reducing bias. While bagging is useful for reducing overfitting, boosting tends to provide more accurate models with better generalization.

110. What is data augmentation in deep learning?

Answer: Data augmentation is a technique used to artificially increase the size and diversity of a training dataset by applying transformations such as rotation, flipping, scaling, and cropping to the existing data. It is especially useful in image processing and deep learning tasks to prevent overfitting and improve model robustness. Libraries like Keras and PyTorch provide built-in functions for data augmentation. This approach helps models learn more generalized features by exposing them to varied input examples.

111. What is model drift in data science?

Answer: Model drift refers to the degradation of model performance over time due to changes in data distribution or real-world conditions. It occurs when the environment or input data evolves, making the original model assumptions invalid. Model drift can be detected through monitoring metrics and comparing recent predictions against historical trends. Retraining the model with updated data or using online learning techniques can help mitigate the effects of drift and maintain model accuracy.

112. What is outlier detection and why is it important?

Answer: Outlier detection is the process of identifying data points that significantly deviate from the rest of the dataset. These anomalies can indicate data entry errors, fraud, or rare events. Detecting outliers is important for maintaining data quality and improving model performance. Techniques such as Z-score, IQR (Interquartile Range), DBSCAN, and Isolation Forest are commonly used. Proper handling of outliers ensures robust and accurate analysis in data-driven decision-making.

113. What is data lineage and its role in data governance?

Answer: Data lineage refers to the life cycle of data, including its origin, transformations, and final usage. It provides a visual representation of how data flows through various systems and processes. In data governance, data lineage is crucial for ensuring transparency, compliance, and trust in data. It helps in auditing, impact analysis, and troubleshooting data quality issues. Tools like Apache Atlas and Collibra help track data lineage in complex data ecosystems.

114. What is GPU acceleration and why is it used in data science?

Answer: GPU (Graphics Processing Unit) acceleration leverages parallel processing capabilities of GPUs to speed up computations, especially in tasks involving large datasets or complex mathematical operations. It is widely used in deep learning, image processing, and high-performance computing. Frameworks like TensorFlow and PyTorch support GPU training for neural networks, significantly reducing training time. GPU acceleration is essential for real-time analytics and applications that require rapid processing of large-scale data.

115. What is a confusion matrix used for in classification tasks?

Answer: A confusion matrix is a tool that summarizes the performance of a classification model by showing the number of true positives, true negatives, false positives, and false negatives. It helps compute various metrics such as accuracy, precision, recall, and F1-score. By providing detailed insight into prediction errors, confusion matrices are essential for evaluating classification models, especially when dealing with imbalanced datasets where traditional accuracy may be misleading.

116. What is cross-entropy loss in classification?

Answer: Cross-entropy loss is a commonly used loss function for classification problems. It measures the difference between the predicted probability distribution and the actual class labels. Lower values indicate better predictions. Cross-entropy is particularly effective for multi-class classification tasks, as it penalizes incorrect predictions more severely. It works by computing the negative log-likelihood of the true class given the predicted probabilities, encouraging the model to assign high probability to the correct class.

117. What is ensemble averaging in machine learning?

Answer: Ensemble averaging is a technique where multiple models are trained independently, and their outputs are averaged to produce a final prediction. It is used to reduce model variance and increase stability. For classification, this may involve averaging probabilities, while for regression, it averages numerical predictions. Ensemble averaging is simple yet powerful, often leading to improved performance compared to single models, especially in competitions or real-world scenarios where accuracy is critical.

118. What is A/B testing in data science?

Answer: A/B testing is a statistical method used to compare two versions of a system (A and B) to determine which performs better. It is widely used in web development, marketing, and product design to test changes in features, layouts, or content. By dividing users randomly into two groups and analyzing their responses, A/B testing provides data-driven insights into user behavior. It helps in optimizing performance, increasing engagement, and making informed business decisions.

119. What is a hash function and its role in big data?

Answer: A hash function is a mathematical algorithm that converts input data into a fixed-size string of characters, typically used for indexing and retrieving items in databases. In big data, hash functions are used in distributed systems for partitioning, deduplication, and fast data retrieval. Hashing ensures efficient storage, secure data comparison, and load balancing across nodes. Hash-based techniques are foundational in systems like consistent hashing in distributed file systems and MapReduce frameworks.

120. What is online learning in machine learning?

Answer: Online learning is a machine learning paradigm where the model is updated continuously as new data becomes available, instead of training on the entire dataset at once. It is suitable for real-time applications like stock prediction, recommendation systems, or fraud detection. Online learning algorithms process data one instance at a time, making them efficient for scenarios with limited memory or evolving data streams. Algorithms such as stochastic gradient descent support online learning naturally.

121. What is the difference between structured, semi-structured, and unstructured data in Big Data?

Answer: Structured data is highly organized and easily searchable using traditional relational databases, characterized by rows and columns (e.g., SQL tables). Semi-structured data lacks the rigid structure of relational data but contains tags or markers to separate data elements, making it easier to analyze than unstructured data (e.g., JSON, XML). Unstructured data has no predefined format and includes formats like videos, audio files, emails, and social media posts. Understanding these distinctions helps data scientists choose appropriate storage, processing, and analysis techniques in Big Data ecosystems.

122. What role do metadata play in Big Data management?

Answer: Metadata, often referred to as "data about data," provides contextual information about data sets, such as their origin, structure, time of creation, and usage history. In Big Data environments, metadata is crucial for managing, cataloging, and retrieving data efficiently. It enhances data discoverability, supports data lineage tracking, and facilitates compliance with data governance policies. By providing insights into data structure and meaning, metadata helps in automating workflows and improving interoperability between systems, making it a key component of Big Data infrastructure.

123. How does anomaly detection work in Data Science applications?

Answer: Anomaly detection involves identifying data points that deviate significantly from the normal pattern or behavior in a dataset. Techniques include statistical methods, clustering algorithms (like DBSCAN), and machine learning approaches such as Isolation Forests and Autoencoders. In Data Science, anomaly detection is widely used in fraud detection, network security, system health monitoring, and predictive maintenance. By uncovering outliers, it enables proactive measures to prevent failures or malicious activities. Successful implementation depends on well-defined normal behavior and proper selection of detection algorithms based on data characteristics.

124. What are the main differences between batch and stream processing in Big Data?

Answer: Batch processing handles large volumes of data collected over a period, processing them together in scheduled intervals. It is ideal for operations that do not require real-time results, such as monthly reports or historical trend analysis. Stream processing, on the other hand, deals with continuous data flows and processes data in real-time or near real-time. It is suited for applications like fraud detection, real-time analytics, and IoT sensor monitoring. While batch processing is typically more cost-efficient, stream processing offers lower latency and faster decision-making capabilities.

125. Why is scalability important in Big Data and how can it be achieved?

Answer: Scalability in Big Data refers to a system's ability to handle increasing amounts of data or traffic without performance degradation. As data grows in volume, velocity, and variety, scalable systems ensure continued efficiency and reliability. Scalability can be achieved horizontally by adding more machines (nodes) to a system or vertically by upgrading the hardware of existing machines. Technologies like Hadoop, Spark, and cloud platforms (AWS, Azure) support scalable architectures. Ensuring scalability is essential for accommodating business growth, maintaining user experience, and reducing infrastructure bottlenecks in data-intensive applications.

9 789369 720

Printed at Repro India Ltd.